The Underground Stream

The Underground Stream

New Life Styles and the Antinomian Personality

Nathan Adler

HARPER TORCHBOOKS
Harper & Row, Publishers
New York, Evanston, San Francisco, London

In somewhat different form a portion of Chapters 2 and 3 was published as "The Antinomian Personality: The Hippie Character Type" in *Psychiatry,* vol. 31 (1968). Copyright by the William Alanson White Psychiatric Foundation. Reprinted by permission.

Another part of those chapters appeared originally as "Kicks, Drugs and Politics" in *The Psychoanalytic Review,* vol. 57 (1970). It is here reprinted by permission.

THE UNDERGROUND STREAM:
NEW LIFE STYLES AND THE ANTINOMIAN PERSONALITY

 For information address Harper & Row, Publishers, Inc., 10 East 53rd Street, New York, N.Y. 10022. Published simultaneously in Canada by Fitzhenry & Whiteside Limited, Toronto.

First TORCHBOOK edition published 1972.

LIBRARY OF CONGRESS CATALOG CARD NUMBER: 72–83620

STANDARD BOOK NUMBER: 06–131683–0

Designed by Ann Scrimgeour

For Judith, Marianna, and Elisa, from whom I learn

Contents

The belief that the evil world as we know it, so full of temptation and corruption, will come to an end one day and will be replaced by a purer and better world, originates in the apocalyptic outlook of the prophets of the Old Testament. It is promulgated in the Christian idea of the Kingdom of God, which the earlier Christians expected in their own time, and it lingers as a passionately turbulent stream, dammed up and hidden by the efforts of the church, but recurrently appearing on the surface of history through the teaching and action of heretical sects.

—*Edward A. Shils*

Foreword

College editors, in the autumn of 1971, observed a turn away from drugs. They pronounced the end of the love generation, the generation of the innocent and the "stoned" flower children. Abbie Hoffman, *enfant terrible* and Yippie leader, has cut his hair and now advises young people to register and vote.

In less than a decade the enthusiasm of the first days of Haight-Ashbury has precipitated into depression, and that new magnetic Bohemia has collapsed into a grim, dreary, and violent slum. Discouraged and indifferent students can no longer be mobilized to stop the war or to change the structure of the campus. Two leading rock and roll stars died of drug overdose. Tim Leary, a refugee, fights extradition from Switzerland. The murders at Altamont followed hard on the promise of Woodstock.

During this time the drug culture has diffused from the college campus to the junior high and the elementary school. Veterans return from the Indochina wars, not the anticipated militant political leaders, but the new wave of heroin addicts. Although the use of LSD, which approached 10 percent on some college campuses, now seems to have slackened, the use of marijuana, is consistently reported to be around 75 percent on many high school and college campuses, in spite of reports that drug use now appears to be less salient.[1]

But the drug culture and counterculture are not limited to the hippies or even to the young. Much has been co-opted by the very system it set out to deride. Even the corporate ads in the college press no longer suggest that one joins the company to get rich or to aspire to great achievement. Instead, they emphasize the pleasures of working with someone else, of thinking and producing as a member of the team. These ads suggest that working for the company is to join a big happy group where one is free to dream, to improvise, and to work without restraint and where one can *communicate.*

Much of "the scene" has been corrupted and commercialized. It is not easy to distinguish culture from "counterculture." Drug and sexual evangelism are evident in both, and they share the same smorgasbord of pills. The young spend Saturday evenings at body-painting parties, while their elders support topless and bottomless theater and bars.

The world of technology and reason contrasts with the neo-romantic world of sensation, intuition, subjectivity, flight from science, and the assertion of antirational and anti-intellectual values. Against positivism, empiricism, rationality, skepticsm are arrayed enthusiasm, youth, "experience," innocence, purity, and nature. Alienation is to be resolved by new rituals and by renewed sacraments.

[1] Associated Press, Oct. 4, 1971, *San Francisco Examiner,* p. 15.

It is not coincidental that Hesse has become the poet laureate of this generation and the best seller in the campus bookstores. This generation resonates in sympathy with the anxious world of the Weimar Republic. Erich Heller has remarked that the modern mind speaks German.[2] Central to the neoromantic values of the counterculture is a configuration that seems to have appeared typically in Germany and that I see as a German disease, engendered by the complex of many principalities and a tardy unified national identity. It is a product of the German language with its ambiguous and allusive global nouns which impell German businessmen to acknowledge that business letters are most clearly written in English.

Where other languages construe the world as process and interaction and feedback, the German typically construes the world as a duality of world and mind: the object (*gegenstand*) is that which literally stands "over against" and too often the bridge is down between the interior introspective experiences and the experiences and events of the world outside. He is a prisoner locked in the Iron Maiden of his skin, and whether messages get in or out remains problematic. The German is preoccupied with essences and with the phenomenal and seems to sense more than others how much reality is constituted and made by categories and how protean and unstable these may be.

Phenomenology as a reduction or analysis of reality into its constituent mosaic bits in consciousness has been an intense preoccupation of German philosophers like Husserl and Heidegger. It took the drug scene and the drug world to make Everyman a phenomenologist, to demonstrate that sophisticated, complex, elaborate procedures of analytic reduction could become a mass-produced consumer product--bending the texture of reality and making accessible mystic and pantheistic fusions

[2] Erich Heller, *The Artist's Journey Into the Interior* (New York: Random House, 1965).

and reductions without the philosophers' and religious leaders' sense of control.

Although there are common elements in the protests of young and old against the mechanization of relationships, there are important differences. The bridges are down between fathers and sons. The fathers are products of the Depression and the search for security, of the two world wars and the shadow of the mushroom cloud, of the cold war, of lost dreams and confused shibboleths, and of the new prosperity, mobility, and the technocratic expansion that replaced the anticipated postwar economic collapse. The youth are products of the new American invention of childhood and adolescence divorced from society and productive labor. They live in the brave new world where adolescence has no function other than to age. They have neither work nor a role, other than that of consumers of brand names and kicks, draftees, or students marking time. Despite the fact that youth now constitutes half or more of the population, they are the new outsider—the adolescent as nigger in whom we begin to see the threat, the danger, the appetite, and the violence of our own projected wishes.

Today's youth are also the product of a world in which the extinction of the human race and the psychotic's dream of world destruction have become a real possibility. Population Council studies of the population explosion estimate that the human race has perhaps 35 years. When ecologists warn that we are poisoning our soil, water, and air, youth hears and is concerned. They are the product of a world in which violence is part of the daily fare. They see prisoners of war knifed and shot before their eyes on evening television broadcasts.

Reacting against such threats and overwhelming problems they anticipate with dread apocalyptic doom, escape into a nostalgic Arcadian retreat, seeking to reestablish rural values at a time when the family farm can no longer be self-sufficient. The family as service station is replaced by a new tribalism that they suppose reverts to the American Indian model, the West and the Indian world of the late show rather than from the realities of Indian and frontier life. Youth invoke peyote rituals and the New American church, but they do not know or see the implication of the fact that peyotism was a product of Indian defeat and the corruption of reservation life. Castaneda's books seem to infer that peyotism is an integral element in Indian religion.[3] But Don Juan's image of the warrior, his preoccupation with altered consciousness, and the manipulation of illusion and reality are an adaptation to defeat and to marginality. It is the response of the hero herded onto the reservation, the adaptation of the boy who witnessed the massacre of his father.

Lanternari describes the development of peyotism in Indian societies in the middle of the nineteenth century, when after the civil war ended, the victorious federal government undertook the opening of the West.[4] The Plains Indians faced the disruption of their social and cultural world; the buffalo herds had been destroyed and their economy was shattered. Driven from their lands onto alien reservations, they sought through peyote a new way to reorder their world and their relation to it.

After 1870 government policy sought to destroy Indian society by destroying its religion. That policy called for enforced assimilation and acculturation. The survivors were herded onto reservations, exposed to tuberculosis, alcoholism, and the proselytism of Christian missionaries. The peyote cult was a reponse to these pressures; it provided a basis for resistance and for the reaffirmation of Indian values.

The peyote cult was preceded by an earlier religious move-

[3] Carlos Castaneda, *The Teachings of Don Juan; A Yaqui Way of Knowledge* (Berkeley. University of California Press, 1968), and *A Separate Reality: Further Conversations with Don Juan* (New York: Simon & Schuster, 1971).

[4] Vittorio Lanternari, *The Religions of the Oppressed. A Study of Modern Messianic Cults* (New York: New American Library, 1965), p. 90 ff.

ment, the Ghost Dance, which promised liberation and redemption and created a morale which supported uprisings against the whites. Only after the Ghost Dance was discredited, because the Indians had to acknowledge their defeat and come to terms with the pressures of acculturation, did the peyote cult arise. In the place of armed resistance to federal force, the peyote cult counseled introspection and meditation and reaffirmed the Indian Great Spirit to counter the intruding Christian god. It reaffirmed ancient myths and rituals and, as such movements characteristically do, looked back to a golden age, promised salvation to the tribe, consoled the people in weakness and defeat, and established new grounds on which to order their disrupted lives. It created the sanctions for repudiating the culture of the alien white man and the justification to maintain and hold fast to their own.

Aberle, an anthropologist who has studied peyotism among the Navajo, describes its use in rebuilding a bridge of ritual. The peyote experience creates a feeling of the personal significance of both internal and external stimuli, but it is an experience that is sought as part of the search for meaning, not as an end in itself. "Peyote is experienced as a power. . . . One feature seems especially relevant. . . . When a person eats peyote, something external to him proves able to affect his thinking, feelings, perceptions, and behavior."[5]

Aberle reports that the Navajos' use of peyote rarely leads to visions. Though some welcome, induce, and institutionalize visions, they are disvalued by many, who report instead that the use of peyote leads to mild or acute anxiety and depression, followed, as a consequence of the group experience, by a mild euphoria the morning after. According to Aberle, the Navajos find incomprehensible the white man's reports of bliss. They find the taste of peyote bitter and suffer nausea, anxiety, and depression. The use of the drug is structured and surrounded by ritual

[5] David Aberle, *Peyote* (Chicago: Aldine Books, 1966).

performances which are taxing. Use is not motivated by hedonistic goals. The positive feelings of personal significance, the successful grappling with the unpleasant, the shared group experience, and vision as communication with the deity are the desired reactions. Peyote is a medium for common purpose, joint effort, and cure. It separates the Navajos from the intruding white world and supports the assertion of their superiority. It becomes the foundation of a morality advocating abstinence from alcohol, one of the gravest public health menaces on the reservation.

Aberle concludes that peyotism appeals to those who seek cure after crisis, to the disorganized and the unhappy, and to the marginal and the alienated reaching for meaning and purpose in the Navajo ghetto. Among the Navajo today, those who are most involved with peyotism appear to be the individuals who have lost their livestock and their wealth. The peyote cult is an effort to sustain solidarity and to create a new Pan-Indian tribalism. On what grounds can it be synthetically invoked by the heirs of the affluent society? What defeat and disorganization leads them in their quest for a mythic Indian tribalism?

Can we account for the new life styles and make sense of the counterculture? Turning on and dropping out, gay liberation and women's liberation, repudiation of the achievement orientation of the acquisitive society, anti-intellectualism, and the search for new mystic experiences—are these random accidents, capricious happenings? Or is their occurrence a predictable response to specific events, lawful in the sense that there are recurring characteristic regularities throughout history when similar needs induce similar personal and institutional responses. Can we meaningfully explain the effort to establish a new community based on faith and identification with the insulted and the injured, the deviant and delinquent, the poor and the psychotic? Can we make sense of politics as theater, of the gently mocking anarchism that would annihilate the Pentagon by levitation, and of the bombs of the Weathermen? Can we account for the quixotic pixies with their put-ons and happenings, that outrage convention, proclaim the absurd, and opt for passive resistance or the rebellion of the romantic New Left that repudiates established socialist societies as well as the capitalist Establishment? Out of their sense of the futility of political action in an unresponding world, one group says politics is not its bag and wears buttons reading "Chicken Little was right!" The New Left, meanwhile, swings in a wide arc from Byronism to Buonopartism. The May "Revolution" in France in 1968 and the struggle for the People's Park in Berkeley in May 1969 both demanded an anarchic and utopian change of values more than they sought political change. Yet these same groups are susceptible to totalitarian movements, whether they be subservience and submission to a guru or religious leader or fusion with a greater whole that will assuage them by making them part of nature or of the state.

In parts of Melanesia and Africa, cargo cults have developed as a response to the disruption of these societies by contact with the modern world. These enthusiastic movements anticipate a new god who will arrive with ships bearing cargo, endowing them with all the wealth of the Western world. In an inversion of the cargo-cult phenomena (yet perhaps meeting the same needs), some groups disdain the "plastic" and the "rat race" and repudiate parents, pedagogues, and politicians as sellouts, school as irrelevant, and marriage as false. They reject established and customary ways, deny that law is binding when it violates the "natural state" of man, and demand the "civil rights" of drug users and other deviants.

"Creativity," as catchword and as the ideology of bead stringing and tie-dying, expresses a longing for a visible manifestation of deity; restless, rootless youth seek beyond the absconded god for a new revelation. They manipulate a euphoria without joy, a depression without sadness, sex without love and care, and togetherness without sympathy. In a world of democratized seers and visionaries every man becomes his own shaman.

But role changes and shifts continue throughout the decade: Flower children become political; diggers desert the city for armed communes; love children manufacture bombs; and acid heads turn into Jesus Freaks. Middle-class Jewish and Christian students seek in astrology and Tarot, in Zen and Yoga, in meditation and macrobiotic diets, in monkish shaven pates and saffron Hare Krishna gowns, and in discarded Air Force jackets and epaulets a transcendence that will transport them from worn and tired roles toward the new selves they wish to become. Mystic and erotic, ascetic and libertine, demanding self-actualization and transcendence, they seek in spiritual exercises and in hyperactivity and overstimulation to establish some ground for the self, some membership they can willingly affirm. Their negativism is adaptive. The current ethos, enmeshed in a dualism that separates good from evil and god from world, grows out of the fragmentation of experience and relationship. The reemergence of interest in the occult and the fantasies of flying saucers, floods, and earthquakes project the inner breakdown they feel.

There is an affirmation as well as a negation in their behavior. In repudiating established roles and in groping toward new grounds for identity, the various cults and sects of the counterculture—at least those which have not been coopted—seek to confirm and give status to roles that are being improvised outside conventional folkways. They claim that they confirm the real and true self rather than some external authority and its accredited roles. To be emancipated from convention and from what is offered as common sense or invoked as law, destiny, or fate requires a new group as a source of support if disengagement and reorientation are to be achieved.

Since the issues are about values, it is difficult to talk about them without falling into a partisan camp. Words like "drugs" and "drug culture" are negatively loaded. They make automatic, invidious distinctions which connote "evil," "strange," and "illegal," and they invoke a distance that suggests "not me" rather than "like me."

The language of those committed to the new life styles is equally immersed in polemic. They maintain that an analytic and detached assessment is not possible and that their experience can only be known by those engaged in it. They dismiss as mere arid thinking, which vitiates and fragments involvement and experience, any effort to objectively examine their acts. They maintain that drug use is not evil and that it can produce psychic rebirth, bring new insights and pleasures, intensify feelings, and renew an automated world. They challenge the charge that they are alienated. To be alienated, they say, is to wish to be elsewhere, at another place or time, to wish to be other than oneself. They affirm, "Here I am in the here-and-now, letting it all hang out."

I am partisan. I am partisan for rationality, for all that extends the range of consciousness and defends the intellectual tradition. I am partisan in repudiating the occult and the superstitious, and I assume that to repudiate these one need not deny the place of the demonic in human experience or deny the attempt to account for it reasonably. One can reject scientism without rejecting science, support a humanistic ethos without ecstasy, which means literally to stand outside oneself, or enthusiasm, which means literally to be filled with gods. Enlightenment is other than illumination, knowing which flees from information to transformation deserts the ancient battle between cognition and the gnostic, the war in which as it has been said, Athens—the world of reason—must be recovered from the occult and enthusiastic world of Alexandria again and again.[6]

I have remarked on the ancient distinctions between cognition as a way of knowing and orienting to the world and gnosticism as another kind of knowing by inspiration and by revelation and intuition. These alternate ways of orienting to the world recur in many places and times.

[6] Peter Gay, *Weimar Culture, The Outsider as Insider* (New York: Harper & Row, 1968), quotes Warburg's celebrated formula.

Gnosticism has taken root in the ancient world, in primitive nonliterate societies. It is one of the central arguments of this book that in our current secular setting the conditions that produce gnostic modes of orienting to experience have produced in the new life styles these characteristic modes of adjustment and response. The early history of the church and its institutions during the first four centuries of the Christian era is a history of the struggle with gnostic values and "heresies" by the early church fathers.

As a mode of orientation, it expresses a direct and personal illumination and rejects control and mediation by established institutions. In this sense gnostic behavior and a gnostic orientation express social and political values that repudiate established ways and are therefore called antinomian, that is, against the lawful or legitimate institutions of the particular society. This does not imply that any revolutionist is by definition gnostic and antinomian. Antinomianism and gnosticism imply the centrality of anti-intellectual and antirational values that derive from a dualistic view of the divine and the corrupt, of good and evil. Protestantism and Marxism, for example, articulate antinomian and gnostic components and also affirm commitments opposed to the gnostic and the antinomian. This orientation can be expressed in both character styles of asceticism and denial or of libertinism and repudiation of limits.

Today, as in the ancient world, Athens wars with Alexandria again. The chapters that follow are an effort to make a partisan but an objective case about this war. I propose to present views I have developed over the last ten years in an effort to understand the drug scene and to comprehend its forms and structures. I cannot accept these events as a function of new technologic breakthroughs. I recall too many instances in history when the same roles and styles appeared. On the other hand, I recall that the charges now leveled against marijuana as an agent of disruptive behavioral change has in the past been leveled at other substances. Tobacco, for example, at the time of the Cromwell Republic in 1650 was deemed to be the corrupter that incited the licentious behavior of the Ranters. Its use was believed to enhance lust and to induce mystic states in which one could experience the impulses of the Holy Spirit. The epigraph by Edward A. Shils suggested to me a way to understand the drug scene and the counterculture. The underground stream as a metaphor for the forces now manifest makes possible the development of a theoretical framework which can order and integrate facts and artifacts, mannerisms and fashions.

Some of the material that follows was presented in a different form to many audiences over the past five years.[7] During that

[7] In somewhat different form and with shifting emphases, the material was presented before audiences and in the following journals:
"Campus Drug Culture," *Per Se,* (1966), pp. 38–41.
"The Use of Drugs and the Manipulation of the Self," *Issues in Criminology,* 2, 1 (1966): pp. 125–136.
"The Drug Scene as a Neo-Gnostic Social Movement," Proceedings, Institute on the Use of Non-Narcotic Drugs, June 28, 1967, Southern Illinois University.
"The Antinomian Personality: The Hippie Character Type," *Psychiatry* 31, 4 (1968), pp. 325–338.
"Ethics, Ethos and Actualization: The Paradigm of the Antinomian Therapies," a paper presented at the Symposium, Drugs and Hippies: Education, Counselling and Therapeutic Strategies, American Psychological Association, San Francisco, August 31, 1968, and published in *Issues of Criminology* 5, 1.
"Themes for an Exhibition," Drug Conference, Smithsonian Institution, Washington, D.C., Nov. 11, 1969.
"Kicks, Drugs and Politics," *Psychoanalytic Review,* 57, 3 (1970), pp. 432–441.
"Drug Abuse As the Manipulation of Body Image, Sensibility and Self: The Antinomian Personality as Tuned Organism," Conference on Drug Use and Drug Subcultures sponsored by Center for Studies of Narcotics and Drug Abuse of NIMH and Haight-Ashbury research project, Mt. Zion Hospital. Department of Psychiatry, Feb. 17, 1970.
"Ritual, Release and Orientation: The Maintenance of the Self in the Antinomian Personality," Conference on Marginal Religious Movements in America Today, Princeton University, April 15–17, 1971 in *Pragmatic Religions: Contemporary Religious Movements in America* (Princeton, N.J.: Princeton University Press, 1972).
"Psychedelic or Psychotoxic," *California's Health,* 29, 5 (1971), pp. 12–14.

time my views have changed in some ways. My earlier critical emphasis has been modified, and I have come to see the drug culture not only as the abdication from political action, but also, in its positive and adaptive components, as an effort to resanctify and renew experience. The movement is not homogeneous. A large part has been co-opted by the Establishment. Boutiques and the record industry in the name of the new life styles have become big business, welcomed by *Fortune* Magazine for introducing new products and revitalizing the market as in other times the Franciscans co-opted the Beghards and the Quakers channelled an innocuous assimilation of the Ranters. The new lifestyles can be used both to support the system and to subvert it.

Individuals within this movement are also not homogeneous. Categories force us into making general statements, yet such a class delineation as drug users contains a complex masking different populations. There may be a significant difference between the cultivated brandy sniffer and the derelict on skid row, yet to acknowledge this difference is not to deny that alcoholism is a major public health problem. On the other hand, it is possible that the insistence on this difference is the consolation we offer ourselves and that the brandy sniffer and the derelict may in some cases represent different locations on the same continuum—the difference, say, in the vicissitudes of stress or the differences in some instances of a history of drunkenness of five years or of twenty.

In the same way, some marijuana users may be curious experimenters who see pretty colors, become bored, and turn to more rewarding involvements in their daily life; or, like the brandy connoisseur, casual smokers of a "joint" after dinner. Others may acknowledge that use leads to increasing tolerance and decreasing satisfaction, impelling them to turn to hashish, peyote, cocaine, and the amphetamines. The existence of these recreational users who successfully manage the psychedelic drugs without loss of control cannot gainsay that the burgeoning drug culture of the last decade has become a major public health problem, and that saffron-robed monks of Hare Krishna, Jesus freaks, the confusion and shifting boundaries of sex roles and taboos express critical stresses and challenges to existing institutions and raise questions about their viability.

In the pages that follow I wish to clarify and to find the operational substance for the newly coined word "psychedelic" and to assess the validity of the imputed pharmacologic effects. Does the new technology differ from other ways of altering behavior and consciousness? This question leads us to examine the social context of the current apocalyptic epidemic and to seek out earlier instances of it.

My basic argument, in citing such instances, is to maintain that we are not dealing merely with historical analogies. Rather, we are attempting to make the case for psychohistory and to explicate the relationship between external rituals and institutions and the internal modification of bodily perception and sensations and the means by which these are used to construe and stabilize the sense of a self. Sensibility and personality are the public and the private faces of the same ongoing process. To make this case, I turn from the social and historical study to review the role of the body image and to see how this perception, as well as information from the outside world, is used in making and modifying the experience of the self. Finally, I discuss some of the newer therapies as an expression of the same antinomian orientation that surfaced in the hippie culture from the enduring underground stream.

The history of that underground stream and of the antinomian personality who rides it is a long-term study. It can be traced through the centuries from the gnostics in Babylon to the Manicheans in declining Rome, from the Albigensians of the medieval world to the Waldensians of the Renaissance, from the Anabaptists of the Reformation to the Ranters of Cromwell's time. Within a generation of the founding of the American colonies in the seventeenth century, New England carried the antinomian current. Heretics, witches, and modern hippies continue that same gnostic and antinomian stream.

To suggest that history can help us understand the phenomena of the last decade frequently provokes resentment. It is misunderstood as a patronizing dismissal, implying only that we are dealing with stale issues that we have faced before. To some it seems to convey the idea that since there appears to be nothing new, the new ethos and the criticism made by these cults is without merit. They see an historical model as one that implies neither consolation nor hope. For them it suggests exact correspondence and eternal repetition. On the contrary, it seems to me that a historical model emphasizes that behavior has its own laws and implies the possibility that one can learn from history and that man can transcend and remake himself.

We tend to teach and relate history as if only the dominant traits—"the successful ones"—ever existed. Yet just as today we see the new existentialism side-by-side with systems theory and operationalism, so theosophy and mysticism flourished during the Enlightenment. Side-by-side with the rationalism and the humanism of the Renaissance, laymen in Genoa, rejecting the scholastics and returning to patristic sources, set up Societies of Divine Love. The Capuchins, reacting against both scholasticism and humanism, became hermits, refusing to own more than three books and receiving from the Pope a dispensation permitting them to grow beards.

With each shift in power and technology and in the spatial range and technological resources of the surrounding world, dualistic adaptive modes have arisen for relating to that new world. Sputnik and the exploration of the moon have again pushed out the boundaries of the secular world and deranged the sacred. Man is confronted again with his power and his helplessness, with the banality of exhausted forms and the need to renew and make sacred the universe.

The study of the social and historical context of character

structure, personality formation, and sensibility is barely begun. I offer the papers that follow as themes and variations for such a work. More than the tendentious preoccupation with immediate concerns, these papers point to a wider view that seeks to account for what Ortega y Gasset has called the metanoid maneuver—the recurrent strategy of conversion in crisis, the reversion into the self, the manipulation and amplification of sensation, the uses of nakedness, diets, innocence, and violence, and the ascetic and libertine strategies which have been repeated so many times in history.[8]

[8] Jose Ortega y Gasset, *Man and Crisis* (New York: Norton, 1962).

"What a curious feeling," said Alice. "I must be shutting up like a telescope!" And so it was indeed: she was now only ten inches high, and her face brightened up at the thought that she was now the right size for going through the little door into that lovely garden. First, however, she waited for a few minutes to see if she was going to shrink any further: she felt a little nervous about this; "for it might end, you know," said Alice to herself, "in my going out altogether, like a candle. I wonder what I should be like then?"

—Alice's Adventures in Wonderland
Lewis G. Carroll

I. Psychedelic Hoax and Pharmacological Fallacy

The quest for the magic potion and the journey down the rabbit hole return perennially. It is a little more than a hundred years since Jacques Joseph Moreau at the Hôpital de Bicetre first used hashish as a curative agent. In his enthusiasm and zeal he introduced the drug to Theophile Gautier who founded Le Club des Haschischins, which diffused drug culture into the bohemian and intellectual worlds of Paris. The hemp derivative was hailed, as LSD in our time, for its hallucinogenic and psychotomimetic qualities. In the name of science, creativity, mind expansion, and exploration of the inner world, coteries like our contemporary cults performed the rites and asserted the ideology of the "psychedelic" experience.

Drugs and drug users incite fascination and dismay more often than they induce reasonable study. Statements by legislators, judges, and law enforcement officers frequently tell more about their fantasy world and their dread of potions and bodily pollution than they reveal about the verified effects of the specific drugs, the persons upon whom they act, the settings in which they are effective, and the social milieu of which they are a part.

In the United States, in this century at least, since the Harrison Act reassigned addictive behavior from patient to deviant role, drug users characteristically have been found among the marginal minority groups who are coping with the problems of assimilation and adaptation to new urban environments. Each wave of immigration has cast up a new deviant, drug-using population.

Suburbia and the campus represent new settings and new recruits. An orientation to drugs, rather than alcohol, may be a signal of other modifications in middle-class personality as it adapts to changing metropolitan society. Cultures can be differentiated by modal behavior, characteristically oriented to alcohol or to drugs,[1] depending upon whether the threats to the self are perceived as originating inside the person or outside. Excitement and attack or withdrawal and retreat are alternative modes of adaptation to stress. Does our society at this time encourage individuals to renounce active for passive solutions or compel a shift in anchorage for the maintenance and defense of the self?

What developmental and social factors account for the choice of active or passive modes of response? What are the differences

[1] G. Morrison Carstairs, "Daru and Bhang: Cultural Factors in the Choice of Intoxicant," *Quarterly Journal of Studies in Alcoholism,* XV (1954), pp. 76–82. Campus users of marijuana and LSD differentiate themselves from the alcohol-using fraternity people in clothes, politics, values, and overt aggression. "Fraternity people drink we don't." an informant told me. Addicts speak contemptuously of alcoholics as "lush heads" who lie down in the gutter. However, this campus differentiation has changed over the years.

between the lower-class junkies as retreatists and the middle-class and professional elite now making the journey to the interior? Does this behavior have the same meaning in both classes? How shall we understand current adolescent drug games? Is this merely Davy Crockett grown older, seeing in a world of more limited opportunities new ways to define and assert his masculine role and achieve status among his peers? Is it the exploration of new frontiers and challenges in the urbanized, corporate ecology that leaves little scope for initiative and individual choice. Does going west now mean turning inside? Or, do the new precocious role-demands made on contemporary adolescents and their earlier confrontation with sexuality force them into drug culture? Do they take "chicken medicine"[2] to overcome timidity and the fear of excitation?

To be high is not to experience something transcendent and extrapersonal. Rather, it is to be able to attribute the apprehended experience to a factor external to the responsible self, to take distance by making the experience a function of an outside agent, instead of one's own. The drug user attributes his internal stimuli to the drug. His aggression, hostility, sexuality, or perversion both fascinate and repel him. He wants to succumb but fears emotional storms and dissolution. Quiescence can save him from action. The experience of fusion and union with the threatening object breaks down the boundaries between the object and the self and overcomes the threat. Drugs become the medium for mastering anxiety. To let go and be high is to play at dissolution and yet, through self-administration, maintain control.[3] Our technocratic age, where the consumer is encouraged to believe that self-esteem and social worth can be manipulated and modified by

[2] Solomon Cohen, Chief of the Adolescent Clinic, Kaiser Foundation Hospital, San Francisco, coined the phrase.

[3] A drug patient commented, "I have my hand on the switch. It is safe to have feelings." A heroin addict reported his fear of pedophile impulses when he was not "turned-on."

packaged products, that tranquilizers, stimulants, gadgets, and techniques can bring about changes in the self, supports the drug-user's do-it-yourself shamanism that engineers ecstasy and delivers instant sartori.

The psychedelic mystique refers to psychotoxic procedures for achieving altered states of consciousness. But there are many ways of altering states of consciousness. Among them are conversion, brainwashing, techniques of induction into the marines, religious retreats, Loyola's spiritual exercises, Stanislavsky's sense memory exercises which are derived in their turn from yoga exercises, and even parachute jumping and mountain climbing. It is important to identify the common factors in meditation, prayer, spiritual exercises, hypnosis, trance, and sensory overloading whether by massage, naked therapy, or manipulation of visual images and sounds, and the effects of pharmacological agents that modify perception, create hyperesthesia and paresthesia, and alter states of awareness.

Technological solutions are offered for what has been achieved at other times by fasting, high fever and sickness, tattooing, and changes in hair fashions, costumes, and beards—procedures that have proved to be as useful and effective in setting the boundaries and construing the identity of the individual in his field. Today chemical focusing of the person is only one way of constituting and maintaining the self. And within the psychedelic politics of pleasure and desublimation, rituals of massage, contact, and "encounter" are as important as drugs in tuning in or tuning out.

It may be that this epidemic diffusion of drug awareness and drug use is the first step in wider public acceptance of the control of mass behavior by means of chemical manipulation. We may be on our way to engineering that brainwashed, compliant, docile consumer and happy robot of the automated world of 1984. Chemical management of people can be more reliable than the techniques of advertising. It can produce the illusion of autonomy and self-assertion while actually it aborts anger and wish to rebel. It can induce withdrawal, maintain passivity, generate wide-screen images of transcendence and eternity, and evoke the mirage of changed selves, like new models off the assembly line. It is heroin addicts rather than black radicals who are returning from the Indochina wars; some estimate that 50 percent of the returning veterans have been heroin users.

Objectively, what can we say of the status and effects of LSD? It is an experimental drug that has not been licensed or released by the Food and Drug Administration for even professional medical use; it is available legitimately only under strict licensing provisions for experimental purposes. The physiological effects of its ingestion are lowering of thresholds; acute distortions of time, space, color, and depth perceptions; and modifications and sharpening in figure-ground relations and in body image. These effects should be studied for whatever insight they can offer on the structure of pathological function and their relevance for psychotherapy. But findings to date seem to confirm that their is no drug-specific behavioral response in the use of LSD; the behavioral effects are a function of predisposing personality, the situation and the setting in which it is administered, the orientation and expectations of both subject and operator, and the induction procedures involved. Claims have been made that the drug may potentially be useful in therapy with alcoholics. On the other hand, there is some question whether the usual placebo effect and response to any new drug or innovative procedure may not also be involved in these equivocal findings.

Who are the drug users? Are they typically the fringe groups that cluster around any campus, with only a slight intrusion into the actual student body? Are they made up of the school drop-outs? Is the drop-out factor a function of prior drug use? Or are both drug use and dropping out of school concurrent expressions of the same antecedent tension that in another decade would have expressed itself in some other way? Is use limited to particular class and ethnic groups or to specific schools and departments? Or does the use of drugs reflect a cross section of the campus community?

A short time ago it could have been said that drug-using students were in the humanities rather than in the technical schools, in the social sciences more than in the physical sciences, among the commuters and apartment dwellers rather than among fraternity and sorority members. There appeared to be a sharp separation between fraternity alcohol-users and liberal marijuana and LSD-users. But the drug culture has diffused out to the fraternity house and even to the financial-world jet set, Sunday halfbacks, and swingers.

It was once the case that if one wanted to know what the middle class would be doing twenty to thirty years later one listened in on the prison yard and the army stockade. From the prison yard, army camp, or black ghetto new ways and values diffused out into bohemia, to the students, and finally penetrated the middle class. In the process, whether it was drugs, "free love," jazz, or mystic experience, it was attenuated into a middle-brow mass culture. Witness today the reaching for mystic experience that depends on the accoutrements of a dimly lit pad with Indian print bedspreads on the wall, sententious readings of Kahlil Gibran, and vague ruminations about the occult that are neither vocation nor discipline but are a part of the consumer culture's drugstore countertranscendence. The "acid" trip—strobe lights and all—took only two weeks in today's commercialized world to become a Broadway nightclub act.

The Pharmacological Fallacy

We cannot speak of drugs as if the issue were merely the ingestion and incorporation of a chemical substance which invariably elicits the same predictable response. Such an approach distorts the facts, leads to pseudo issues, and creates the base for the futile polemics which have dominated the discussion.

Such a restricted focus is based on a pharmacological fallacy. The consumption of drugs is not merely a physiological event. The drugs we use, whether as beverages, pills, injections, or smoke, exist within a matrix of psychological, cultural, and social values; and it is the roles and meanings of these that we incorporate with the drug. The pharmacological fallacy is the assumption that there is a single, specific drug effect independent of the individual's set or the setting in which the event occurs. There is experimental, clinical, and cultural evidence to repudiate this pharmacological fallacy.[4]

What one uses, in what manner, when and with whom, whether one "drinks like a gentleman," stands at a bar or sits in a dimly lit cocktail lounge, shares in a fraternity beer bust or partakes of a sacrament or a communion, drinks with meals, with men only or in mixed groups, or trips out alone or is accompanied by a trusted guru, is always the election or repudiation of a role, the assertion or rejection of a membership and a commitment. We can distinguish patterns of wine use in France from those in Italy; patterns of drug use in India from those in Pakistan, in the Andes, or among American Indians. We are familiar with differences in drug use between Eskimo men and women, between Mormons and Jews. To introduce a trait complex into a culture—whether it be a steel axe on a South Sea island, "firewater" on a defeated Indian reservation, or marijuana or LSD to urban youth in western industrial society—is inevitably to introduce disruption unless the trait is embedded in a context that sanctions, legitimates, patterns, and controls the social behavior. One cannot legalize or prohibit drug use and abuse by fiat alone without attending to the normative systems that establish the built-in control and that institutionalize both the use and abuse of the drugs.

In this context I have trouble understanding Margaret Mead's

[4] H. Osmond, "Review of Clinical Effects of Psychotomimetic Agents," *Annals, New York Academy of Science,* Vol. 66 no. 3 (1957), pp. 418–434.

advocacy of the legalization of marijuana in this country. She fails to deal with, and as an ethnologist she must, the ways in which institutions and norms in the short run accommodate to legislative fiat. It is one thing to use marijuana in India, Pakistan, or Morocco, where its use is institutionalized like the cocktail hour or wine with dinner, and another to turn on and stay stoned on five or six joints a day, seven days a week as potheads do when they have no norms to structure and ritualize use. It is one thing to use drugs that foster passivity and quiescence in a society in which such values are salient, but it is another to impose them on an activist culture that demands other roles. It is even one thing to get drunk and pass out and another to be strung out on amphetamines (speed) for days on end or to impose hyperactivity on a society already so active and so unable to deal with contemplation.

The remark has been often made that we are already a drugged society, that is, committed to patent medicines, tobacco, alcohol, caffein, tranquilizers, and barbiturates. We can concede this and note not only that alcohol and tobacco are public health problems and that we need not seek new ones, but that at least as problems, the use of these products and the roles they demand are already institutionalized in our culture. It is also noteworthy that despite the argument for the alternatives of marijuana and alcohol, there is increasing evidence that the same people misuse and abuse not one or the other but both. The pothead also becomes the lush. It is the committed acid user who often turns to speed and then exhaustedly seeks in heroin sleep and relief from the hyperstimulants. Despite the arguments that it was only a police myth that marijuana led to the harder drugs, there is mounting evidence that heroin use has invaded populations previously uninvolved in its use.

I am not implying that marijuana is itself a narcotic drug or that it is physically and physiologically addictive like heroin or morphine. It is a mild hallucinogen. But to speak of a chemical substance, isolated from the social and cultural context of its use, is simpler and more naive than, an anthropologist at least, has the right to be.

There is an old saw that the alcohol problem is not in the bottle but in the user. This is equally true of hallucinogens and tranquilizers. One cannot speak sensibly of these drugs without examining the selection and induction process that determines who becomes a user and under what circumstances. One cannot generalize about drug effects without differentiating such issues as types of use—is the use experimental, casual, recreational, or habitual? What stage is the user in? Some curious dabblers try a drug once or twice then go on to more rewarding and gratifying achievements. Others progress through various stages of use and commitment. A distinction must also be made in the subgroup membership of the users. There appear to be patterned differences in the use of hallucinogens, sedatives, tranquilizers, and stimulants that differentiate various subgroups, the roles they fill, and the destinations at which they arrive. Unless one traces out such social networks and fixes the age, ethnic, and religious factors that seem to be involved, one can make no meaningful statement about patterned drug use. Global generalizations belong to the rhetoric of propaganda and politics. They add little to the information on which a responsible public social policy can be developed. Dionysian cultures cannot be legislated into existence. A moral holiday or Mardi Gras cannot become a total way of life. Institutionalized deviance, necessary though it may be, defines the limits of a society rather than its ideal.

Social psychologists have long appreciated that society needs deviance to mark the boundaries of a culture and to separate inside from outside. Casting out the deviant helps those in a society to establish group solidarity and to define its norms. The election of a deviant role is for some individuals a necessary adaptive act. There has been evidence to suggest that the use of marijuana or LSD has been substituted for other criminal behavior by some individuals who can find in such use as effective an activity as they formerly found in adolescent car theft and joy-riding or other petty larcenies. It is possible that legalization of use of marijuana will only induce in such individuals other, more malignant deviant behavior.

The psychotherapist, for example, is not a naïve athletic healer. Before he attempts to dry out and cure an alcoholic or drug addict, he asks what behavior will take the place of the pathological activity. Curing some drunks or junkies may trigger a suicide or a homicide or induce a full-blown paranoia or a totally disabling depression. A wise society provides deviant roles and tries to institutionalize a deviance that is mild and benign. Such deviance, endemic in every society, leaves room for the misfits, the "queer ducks," and the marginal cranks. It also provides for a growing edge of creativity and renewal in every society and is part of the underground stream.

Public concern has been diverted to the use of such hallucinogenic substances as marijuana, mescaline, and peyote. In part, this alarm has reflected distrust at the intrusion of substances alien to our culture. At the same time, the alarm obscures the fact that the problem of drug use is a wider one. Part of the picture is the television image of the American housewife, fretful, harried by noisy children, dreading the arrival of her mother-in-law, and being told by the purring announcer to reach for an Anacin or a Compoz. The message conveyed daily on TV and radio is that problems need not be solved. They can be masked, denied, and transcended by one little pill. In a technological society that offers prefabricated solutions that require neither effort nor adjustment, the youthful drug scene is hardly incongruent.

We have been victimized by a contrived word, "psychedelic," as a mask for what is essentially a psychotoxic process. Coining this word to denote specific drugs and behavioral effects seems to me to relate more to merchandising and advertising techniques than to the deliberations and classifications of the scientist. The implication of introducing such a word was that a unique set of processes was involved that differentiated some drug effects from others.

But it is clear that Humphry Osmond, director of the New Jersey Neuropsychiatric Institute, who coined the word, cannot justify such a claim, since similar effects can be obtained with industrial poisons and other psychotoxic agents. He is making a value discrimination, maintaining that pleasant, benign, and positive responses are to be identified as psychedelic whereas negative responses are to be classified as psychotic or toxic. Osmond said:

> I have tried to find an appropriate name . . . that will include the concepts of enriching the mind and enlarging the vision.
>
> Some possibilities are: psychephoric, mind moving; psychehormic, mind rousing; and psycheplastic, mind molding. Psychezymic, mind fermenting, is indeed appropriate. . . . My choice, because it is clear, euphonious, and uncontaminated by other associations is -edelic, mind manifesting.

This euphonious word was used to describe drugs that included lysergic acid diethylamide (LSD), dimethyltriptamine (DMT), bufotenin, pscilocybin, pscilosin, mescale, tetrahydro-cannabinols (synthetic marijuana), and similar synthetic hallucinogens.

The word "psychedelic" not only limits the response to positive effects, deliberately accentuating optimistic values and seeking to differentiate these from the pejorative implications of labels like psychotomimetic or hallucinogenic, it also is enmeshed in an unexamined philosophy that names and locates mind as thing rather than process. It reenforces science fiction fantasies about mind expansion, and reopens the gate to the tide of superstitions and occult, obscurantist mystification that constantly surge against dikes of rationality that are slowly built and won.

The word "psychedelic" also implies a uniform reaction and masks the fact that responses to these drugs are variable; the positive emphasis blurs or disregards such issues as the identity of the user, his motive and mood, the state of his physical and psychological health, and his expectancy about the drug's effect and the role of this programming in inducing the effect he seeks. In implying unique processes and responses, the word "psychedelic" also blurs problems of dosage, dose standardization, learning, and physiological psychological tolerance as well as the issues of the setting in which the drug is taken and administered. For example, it has been noted that use of drugs in a group setting and with group support leads to fewer negative responses than self-administration of drugs by isolated users.[5] Individuals brought into county hospitals suffering from "bad trips" are likely to be solitary drug users.

The positive emphasis also overlooks that effects such as nausea, increased pulse rate, numbness, hallucination, anxiety, changes in sense perception, and the experience of depersonalization are as frequent in the psychedelic experience as they are with such poisons as carbon monoxide, arsenic, methylbromide, mercury, lead, and such industrial solvents as benzine. Methylbromide, for example, a colorless gas used in the chemical industry as a refrigerant and insecticide, produces euphoria, excitement, visual disturbances, and hypersensitive responses to sound. It also produces tremor, chills, disturbances in body temperature, intensification of sound and sight, dizziness, epileptiform convulsions, and hallucinations. Manganese has toxic effects on the miners who inhale the dust. Manganese dioxide, used in steel alloys, glass and match manufacturing, and dry-cell batteries, is a nerve toxin, which like LSD can produce elements of the good and the bad trip, with languor, sleepiness, mask-like ex-

[5] J. Thomas Ungerleider, Fuller, Fisher, et al, "The 'Bad Trip'—The Etiology of the Adverse LSD Reaction," *American Journal of Psychiatry,* no. 124 (May 1968), pp. 1483–1490.

pression, a low and monotonous voice, muscular twitching, and uncontrollable laughing and crying. Psychic changes are also present with lead poisoning, though sensory disturbances are not common. Mercury poisoning induces depression and anesthesia. In reports of poison effects on auditory and optic nerves, it is not clear whether we are dealing with hallucination or merely with the loss of sensations.

It is clear that the drug effects vary widely and can be modified by physical conditions and by the social setting, which may be suggestive and contagious. It is misleading to single out the word "psychedelic" for drugs that can be both euphoric and anxiety-provoking.

In another paper Osmond and his associates attempt to contrast positive psychedelic experiences with negative psychotic experiences.[6] They argue that psychedelic experiences are voluntary and fail to see that counterphobic and compulsive motivations may be involved. Psychologists recognize that people sometimes run toward that which they fear most. The drug user manages his fear of loss of control by deliberately playing at loss of control.

Osmond and his associates maintain that the psychedelic experience, as contrasted with the psychotic experience, is liberated from time. Such a view fails to appreciate the compulsive quality of the immediacy, the cult of the "here and now," the loss of a future-time perspective, the devaluation of the past, and the sense of timelessness and "eternity," which are elements in the "psychedelic" drug experience. Osmond selects only positive effects and constructs a definition that denies the bad trip, the hidden, and the threatening. He equates the psychedelic with delight, and in his definition, disgust and loathing are assigned to the psychotic. If one construes subhuman forces, these by

[6] M. Siegler, H. Osmond, and H. Mann, "Laing's Model of Madness," *Salmagundi,* a quarterly of the Humanities and Social Sciences, published by Skidmore College, no. 16 (Spring 1971), pp. 84–104.

definition become psychotic; but if one construes a benevolent superhuman source, this achieves the honorific of the psychedelic.

In the psychedelic he finds unity with people and objects; in the psychotic, invasion by people and objects; in one the experience of self, in the other, the fragmentation of self. Such a dichotomous view cannot account for the mystic's loss of the sense of self or his often reported distortion of space and body image. For Osmond the psychedelic experience is preserved for being at one with the world, and he disregards or classifies as psychosis the manic inflation of the ego that can also be a consequence of drug use. He asserts values and predilections that blur rather than discriminate and by the fiat of a definitional game creates the circularity that the psychedelic is benign and good, while the psychotic and the psychotoxic belong to another universe. Thus he is able to maintain that the psychedelic stimulates new fashion and new music and that this is not true of the psychotic or pathologic.

Given this fiat, he is not able to examine the many instances in which the pathological has been associated with the creative. Instances that come at once to mind include Van Gogh's textures, the relation of Cezanne's perspectives to his astigmatism, the metaphorical structure in Zelda Fitzgerald's *Save Me the Waltz*—a list that scrutiny of art history would extensively expand.

The word "psychotoxic" is as negative in its implications as the word "psychedelic" is intended to be positive. Both are loaded words; both intend to manipulate attitudes. The one difference appears to be that the psychotoxic is usually assessed by the effects on organs and their functions, an effect usually noticeable on inspection, whereas the claims for the psychedelic effects are not scientific accounts. They are merely subjective accounts of how these effects seem to the drug user and are themselves symptoms.

It is maintained that the metabolism of psychedelic substances leaves no traces and that psychedelic drugs selectively affect only psychological functions without altering the other major body systems. However, the final word on organic consequences of psychedelics has not yet been said. Signs of organic damage in chronic users may yet be found.

The medical literature, on the other hand, tends to neglect and overlook psychological effects produced by toxins. Because of a physician's orientation to the body and the organ systems, it is often only incidentally that the doctor mentions the psychological effects of industrial poisons. These toxins often affect sight, sound, color, and feelings, and not necessarily in disagreeable ways. A search of the literature reveals little notation of the mental symptoms of poisoning. "Hallucination" is frequently reported but no indication is made of the character, severity, or duration of the hallucinations. Until specific clinical case accounts are obtained from the emergency clinics in major industrial cities, this information will be lost.

One such instance of the commonality of the psychotoxic and the psychedelic came to my attention:

> A self-employed furniture finisher used a paint remover. Directions cautioned against use in an enclosed space and so it was used customarily in the open air where air circulation would carry away the fumes. One day, stripping varnish and stain from a large piece of furniture, it started to rain. He and his associate moved the work into the garage, closed the door against rain, and continued to work.
>
> After a time he began to feel strange and noted that his fellow worker also behaved oddly. He felt light-headed, and extremely tall, the tops of the wall seemed to be slanted forward:
>
> "It seemed as though I were looking through a pair of glasses, each of whose lenses was focused for a different length. This gave a slight distortion of size to whatever I looked at. The rain seemed abnormally loud and insistent. This state did not alarm me but rather amused me very much. I remember that I didn't want to blink as that might

> change the focus of my eyes and send everything back to normal. In spite of this, I felt that the doors must be opened, and I moved in what seemed to me to be very slow motion over to the large double door. After a few minutes in the fresh air, my head cleared, leaving an intense headache and sick stomach. My associate's reaction was more toward a slight distortion of vision and dizziness. Both of us had headaches afterwards.''

The words ''psychedelic,'' ''psychotomimetic,'' ''psychotropic,'' ''psychoactive,'' and ''hallucinogenic,'' it should be clear, are variously used for a set of processes that are also psychotoxic. Toxic psychosis due to gasoline inhalation has been compared to the syndrome resulting from the use of mescaline, LSD, and psilocybin.[7] Psychotomimetic effects have been observed in deliberate toluene inhalation.[8] Psychedelic drug effects overlap those of such drugs as bromides, atropine, barbiturates, cocaine. Continued use of the word ''psychedelic'' rather than ''psychotoxic'' serves the press agent more than the behavior scientist. Hallucination, euphoria, depression, concretion in thinking, modifications in the perception of space, time, and color, and reification of affect (the process by which ideas and names are conceived as real objects) are the familiar phenomena of the drug ''trip'' and are the same psychotoxic effects that are produced by common industrial and household poisons.

One can achieve the same effects by ''shooting'' many bizarre substances—nutmeg, furniture polish, aerosol freezers, airplane glue, and other agents.[9] In the *San Francisco Chronicle* for

[7] E. J. Tolon and F. A. Lange, "Model Psychosis Produced by Inhalation of Gasoline Fumes." *American Journal of Psychiatry* (1964), pp. 120–157.

[8] E. Press and A. K. Dave, "Solvent Sniffing," *Pediatrics,* I 39, 45 (1967); II, *Ibid.* 39, 611 (1967).

[9] O. Marburg and M. Helfand, *Injuries of the Nervous System Including Poisonings* (New York: Veritas Press, 1939).

October 22, 1969, some compulsive users were reported to have been shooting peanut butter and mayonnaise into their veins.

It is ironic to find that engineers and technicians are often the most enthusiastic sponsors of this movement to repudiate or transcend technology and seek to return to "spontaneous" and "natural" freedom by way of chemicals. Is the sorcerer's apprentice attempting to undo his work? Technicians at the National Air Space Administration Space Flight Center, under the sponsorship of the Esalen Institute, present lectures on pantheistic awareness and bioelectric field effects and explore subjective states. Other members of the Esalen staff lecture on technologies of self-control. The word "psychedelic" also invokes technocratic, science fiction fantasies of an expandable brain and the infinite cosmic regress within the brain cell.

The advocates of drug use claim that drugs liberate the mind and heighten creative powers. Their description of the effects of drugs, however, are not scientific accounts of these effects. They are merely subjective accounts of how these effects seem to the drug user. They are themselves symptoms of the use of drugs. Timothy Leary, in his description of brain cells, visualizes space in ways that are characteristic of individuals under the influence of drugs. In the lithographs of Piranesi, the visions of Coleridge or DeQuincy, even in the whodunit *Methinks the Lady*, by Guy Endore, one finds the same spatial manipulation, the play with infinite regression, with limitless expansions and contractions of space that are a product of drug toxicity and the abnormal, heightened tactile sensitivity, or hyperesthesia, that it produces.[10]

It merits comment that Aldous Huxley's enthusiastic report, in the *Doors of Perception*,[11] about his experience of color with the use of mescaline was written by the same man who struggled

[10] Alethea Hayter, *Opium and the Romantic Imagination* (Berkeley, Calif.: University of California Press, 1968).

[11] Aldous Huxley, *The Doors of Perception* (New York: Harper & Row, 1964).

for years with the exercises of the Bates Method in an attempt to overcome his failing sight. Through mescaline he achieved an interior vision which substituted for the objective world he never saw precisely and which was increasingly inaccessible to him. Klüver, a leading psychologist who had been studying the effects of mescal long before the diffusion of the current drug cult, quotes C. R. Marshall's inquiry into the cause of mescal visions.[12] Marshall, in 1937, suggested: "The rods and foveal cones in the eye can look backward and the retinal pigment and the choriocapillary circulation can therefore be seen under certain conditions." It is also significant, in the light of current reports and ruminations by advocates of extrasensory perception about colored auras observed around people and objects that tremble and flicker like flames, an experience also reported with LSD and other hallucinogens, that Klüver remarked that physiologists attempt to account for such visual phenomena by connecting them with secretions on the cornea, moving particles in the vitreous humor, the network of retinal vessels, and states of the cornea and lens. The inclusion of retroretinal structures emphasizes how interior and self-encapsulating this vision, which alters size, shape, color, and form, can become.

The use of drugs that appear to lower thresholds and to create, independent of specific drug effects, a modification in set creates a demand to pay attention because something significant is about to happen, induces changes in the field, enhances contrast effects, and evokes experiences of color. Such effects are also found in the delirium of high fever in measles, malaria, tonsillitis, influenza and in the visual experience that result from hypoglycemia, the lowering of the sugar level in the blood.

Psychedelic vision is like the mirrors in the fun house that distort the image of the body, multiply and duplicate images,

[12] Heinrich Klüver, *Mescal and Mechanisms of Hallucination* (Chicago: Phoenix Books, University of Chicago Press, 1966).

and minimize and maximize the perception of objects in ways that are also achieved by psychotoxic states. In Klüver's language, mescal visions produce monocular and binocular dyplopia, that is double vision in one or both eyes, polyopia, micropsia, and macropsia a multiplication, magnification or reduction of images. Mescal hallucinations modify the perception of forms so that objects can be seen in filligrees and latticework and as chessboards, honeycombs, gratings; space can be distorted into tunnels and funnels and into cones and vessels; and objects can revolve, bend, and whirl into spirals.

These shifts in size and shape and the changes in dimension and intensity can be accounted for in physiological terms. It is a variable response that differs from person to person, from drug trip to drug trip, and from one drug stage to another. To attach cosmic meaning to these events is a presumption. We are more likely confronting here the projection of affect onto the outside world. The response that one thinks he recognizes is his own projected and reflected image. Psychedelic mind expansion and infinite cosmic regress is a product of drug intoxication and of psychotoxic hyperaesthesia that encloses the perceiver inside a set of Chinese puzzle boxes.

II. Antinomianism in History

Man has a limited repertoire of characteristic responses to recurring needs and to crises. Although the metaphors used to describe experience may change, behavior is similar. I am interested not so much in evaluating a specific movement, such as the Shakers' and Quakers' attempts to renew the world, as in making a theoretical and historical examination of the recurring relationship I find between antinomian movements and their stressful social contexts. I hope to demonstrate that historical data are more useful in formulating personality theory and social psychology than are stimulus-response models or learning theory. Attempts to account for "new" life styles, both drop-out and activist, are usually formulated in exclusively contemporary terms and invoke technology or pharmacology. But technology and drugs are merely focuses around which behavioral forms have crystallized out of ever-present, underlying social and psychological processes. Today we couch in technological metaphors issues that formerly were couched in other metaphors—such religious terms as *heresy*, or such aesthetic terms as *romanticism*. Behavioral forms, though differing in particulars within and between periods, nevertheless have a common structural base. I have attempted to account for this base by use of the term *antinomian*.

Antinomian social movements develop in times of transition and crisis, when traditional values come to seem inadequate as a basis for constitution of the self. These movements surface in times of social disequilibrium and critical change, accompany the terror and disruption of plague, famine, and defeat in war. Often these movements offer platforms for career and status-hungry intellectuals who seek to overcome political frustrations. Resenting the ways in which established functionaries and bureaucrats are disproportionately rewarded, these marginal intellectuals deprecate the established system and respond to their frustration by becoming drunk with illusions. Alienated from political and social power, denied access and opposed to the established bureaucracy, they reject its careers and roles and seek sanction in new or revived myths. An apocalyptic ethos of decline, destruction, and renewal is central to their orientation, and they either respond with zeal and hyperactivity or surrender as passive spectators; they may become arrogant supermen and scornful self-actualizers or populists rediscovering the people. They may celebrate their isolation or attempt to overcome it by sentimental improvisations that deny their homelessness.

It is especially noteworthy that women also have found in such periods a breakthrough for their blocked mobility and are often found playing leading roles in heretical movements which support the emergence of matristic values as opposed to the patristic controls of the Establishment.

The roles antinomian movements invoke and the values which

accompany them recur throughout history. They are to be found in the Sixth-century B.C. Orphism, an aftermath of the Peloponnesian War; in the NeoPythagorean movement of the first century, B.C.; in the Neoplatonism of Plotinus in the third century A.D. Gnostic systems surface after disasters. God is felt to have failed in his promise or to have absconded. As Augustine remarked, one lives between two worlds—one dead, the other powerless to be born. Whether it is the fall of Jerusalem or the cargo-cult of a contemporary preliterate society, the gnostic maneuver becomes the adaptive response.

If one scans such phenomena as the decline of Rome and the heretical movements prevalent at the time,[1] if one follows the various streams that led to the development of nationalism and that culminated in the Reformation,[2] and if one scutinizes the values, roles, and social changes that developed as a response to the industrial revolution, the French Revolution, and the Napoleonic Wars, which usually are identified as the romantic movement in Germany, England, France and Middle Europe,[3] one finds the recurrence of similar value systems. In all a common theme appears—one which is manifested again in today's hippie movement. All show identical modes of adaptation as a response to similar kinds of social stress. One need not imply an eternal return as Nietzsche did or assume a theory of historical cycles as the late seventeenth-century Neapolitan philosopher of history, Giovanni Battista Vico, did to maintain that there are historical regularities or to argue that social crisis in different historical periods may produce similar values and modes of adjustment.

It is an adjustment impelled to flout authority or to surrender to it, to renounce the system or to yield to an implacable destiny

[1] E. R. Dodds, *Pagan and Christian in an Age of Anxiety* (New York: Cambridge University Press, 1965).

[2] George H. Williams, *The Radical Reformation* (Philadelphia: Westminster Press, 1962).

[3] J. L. Talmon, *Romanticism and Revolt: Europe 1815–1848* (New York: Harcourt Brace Jovanovich, 1967).

with self-renunciation. The antinomian, whether manifest as heretic, witch, romantic, drug user, or Jesus freak, denies the legitimacy of the established order and sets about to improvise a new one. Since the antinomians find no congruence in their relationships, perceive the milieu as meaningless, tyrannical, and alien to their purpose, they deem it to be the expression of a brutal, stupid fate. They repudiate and lose themselves or strive to transform and construe new selves. Such seizures and contradictions are experienced as ecstasy, as they seek to be liberated from what they behold as mere illusory appearance and to reaffirm and reinstate their freedom. Such a condition and such goals are formulated as an apocalyptic drama which overcomes the snare of the present and promises an escape from its entrapment.

The specific issues change in place and time. The struggle may be between burghers and feudal lords, between wandering weavers and printers and the entrenched power of monasteries. Today the issue may be faculty autonomy and independence from a board of regents or students' demand for a voice in the making of university policy and personnel decisions. Such issues recall the Renaissance and the Reformation. Issues change, technologies differ radically, and the social classes represent altogether different forces. There are idiosyncratic differences and a wide variability in the responses made. But need we be compelled to choose polarized alternatives, either the unique isolated event or the typical generalization which permits no variability? We need not swing from a world whose meaning is totally established because it is ordered by God to a nihilistic relativism of events devoid of meaning, structure, and significance.

To suggest that there are regularities need not imply that history unfolds in predetermined and inevitable ways nor deny that each generation and people rewrites its past and chooses its answers by a constant process of selection and reinterpretation of prior events. It is not unreasonable to say that events do not exist; rather, they are construed. In the same way that the paleontologist tries to reconstruct the appearance of the dinosaur from the fragment of bone he finds or that the physical anthropologist infers and reconstructs the physical characteristics of societies and cultures from shards and other residual traces, the psychologist and the historian also are engaged in similar tasks. A psychologist, Siegfried Bernfeld, once defined psychoanalysis as a *spurren wissenschaft,* a science of traces. Psychologists and historians share common problems of determining how to evaluate and assess the residual bits of data they obtain and how to use these contemporary signs and traces in the task of reconstruction and inference about a no longer existing event. Both are equally concerned with ways to assess the reliability and validity of the inferences they construct.

Psychohistory is more than the psychobiographic study of a Leonardo or a Luther and more than the demonstration of the place of pathology in a particular person's career. Psychohistory seeks to establish the determinants of sensibility and identity in a particular time and place, to clarify the consequences of specific modes of socialization and the roles to which these lead, and to study the habitat of meaning and value and the cognitive structures which develop within them. Most fundamentally, psychohistory implies the existence of enduring structures as a product of the interaction between person and field.

In our time and in the earlier periods to which I have referred, the recurrence of similar needs and contexts, whether in an ecclesiastical or in a secular setting, has produced similar adaptive techniques that have led to the same personality configuration. Similar needs seem to provoke similar responses. These may take the form of sexual activity, religious exercises, fasting, the ingestion of drugs, or other techniques. These strategies have been invoked again and again: in the gnostic heresies of the third century; in the many sects of the Albigensians, the Cathars, and the Manichaean movements of the medieval world; in the anabaptist movements at the time of the Reformation; after the French Revolution; and during the series of revolutions that followed the Napoleonic Wars. In this century they are also found after the failure of the Russian Revolution in 1905 and after the defeat of Germany in World War I. The responses may be either libertine or ascetic.

There is an apocalyptic sense of the "last days." Individuals renounce family, traditional marriage, and jobs; establish their own small communities and their own new rituals; and affirm sexual libertarianism. Radical changes in styles of dress are often accompanied by exhibitionism. Trances, visions, talking in tongues, possession, and other ecstatic behavior become common. Libertinism often alternates with asceticism, violence with passive resistance, in response to the challenge of temporal power.

Significant psychological data will not be recovered if we limit our attention to circumscribed variables, such as the pharmacological properties of drugs, or if we confine our studies to the peripheral transactions of the human organism.

Psychology has confined itself to a naïve physicalism of stimulus and response in the study of behavior and has not used the study of history as a means of illuminating the dark corners of present-day conduct. In idiographic studies which examine individual biography and pathology, psychologists grudgingly permit a psychohistory, but there still is no indication that they can conceive of a nomothetic enterprise, one whose methods and procedures are designed to discover general laws, as opposed to attempts to understand a particular individual or event, that can make relevant use of historical data. Psychohistory is today confined to the intuitions of *Verstehenpsychologie* and its "understanding" rather than given scope as an explanatory procedure in behavioral studies.

The Relevance of Psychohistory

Even as today's existentialism lives alongside system theory and operationalism, so theosophy and mysticism flourished during the Enlightenment. Even as Columbus sought new western routes to the Indies, Beghards and Waldensians wandered through the streets of Renaissance cities. In the Anabaptist world and in the counterculture of today,[4] despite dissimilarities in each period's dominant cultures, one finds the same millennial fervor of chiliastic movements against the "empire of Babylon"; the same reach for a new man and the redemption of time; similar collective events and charismatic leaders; the same splintering of these movements into groups demanding conformity to the group's identity. In each period are manifestations of an inner discontent with an externally exciting but too changing world. It will be helpful to review and point to similarities in the intellectual, social, political, and economic contexts of varying periods to illustrate our case. Each period manifests similar modes of retreat or of overstimulation for coping with discontent and with a world changing too quickly. In modulating the inner life or stimuli from the world outside, people establish a habitat of sensibility, a range of stimulation, excitement, or withdrawal that becomes characteristic and adaptive for specific social and historical settings. It will be helpful to review and note similarities in the intellectual, social, political, and economic contexts of varying periods to illustrate our case for the function of sensibility.

The Gnostics, Hippies of Religion

The writings of Marcus Aurelius anticipate and document the decline of the Roman Empire. He records the existential anguish familiar in our time. He speaks of man, standing on a knife-edge between two voids, naught but smoke to be blown away. The self is a puppet, a stringed marionette; man is an actor playing roles that are so many external masks. Life was perceived as games, dreams, and deliriums, in the same way that in our time some speak of trips and happenings and even of game theories of war

[4] Erwin Scheuch ed., "Die Wiedertaufer der Wohlstandsgesellschaft, Eine Kritische Untersuchung der Neuen Linken und Ihre Dogmen." (Koln: Markus Verlag, 1968).

and of psychotherapy. In recurring periods the experience of alienation becomes typical for the sensibility of its time. Men feel detached from their roles, events appear unreal—mere formal manipulations, the playing out of charades. The texture of reality is torn, one is separated from rather than invested in one's activity. Cries and queries about "authenticity" arise. The layman who speaks about "games" senses for the first time what the philosophers and phenomenologists have long known—that we construct our worlds—but in speaking of games the novice makes this knowledge his own in a context of dismay and despair.

The Pax Romana was coming to an end in Aurelius' time. The barbarians were at the gates. It was a time of runaway inflation, recurrent epidemics, personal disaster, and sacked cities. There were portents of doom, rumors of invasions from other worlds, and fear of the world's end.

It was in such apocalyptic times that the gnostic heresies arose as social movements.[5] Gnosis refers to knowledge, but not as an analytic and cognitive process. It implies, instead, illumination, revelation, and intuition as the basis of truer, purer, and better knowing. The gnostic heretical cults rejected the authority of church and law and devised new strategies to achieve salvation. These movements rejected the worldly life and turned to the interior self for truth. Scorning established institutions, they insisted on direct and personal access to insight and to God. They defended faculties that they deemed to be superior to reason and to order. Liturgy and ritual had lost meaning for them. They reached out for a pantheistic fusion and unity or for a total escape from the bondage of this evil world. The members of these sects founded utopian communities and colonies and aspired to a self-actualization in which they would free the pneuma, or spirit, from its bondage in the contemptible body. They spoke in tongues, joined cults of love, and sought ecstasy as a steady state.

[5] Hans Jonas, *The Gnostic Religion,* 2d ed. (Boston: Beacon Press, 1963).

The gnostics believed that through spiritual exercises they could achieve union with the Holy Ghost and that for them sin was no longer possible. Therefore they were absolved of obligation to moral law. Libertine excesses degraded both the evil body and the scorned world. In avoiding procreation and rejecting marriage, they hastened release from the fleshly prison and accelerated the return to the Godly spirit. In rejecting all that was worldly, they spurned the ornate in both the rituals and imagery of the church and in their personal lives. They affirmed, instead, a simplification of values, rites, and dress. In their zeal some became ascetic and others turned to libertine indulgences and wilful perversions. It has been suggested that the essence of an idea or an act is to be found in its polar opposite. The libertine as much as the ascetic devalues the world and spends himself the sooner to find release and escape.

These movements distrusted rational analysis and relied on inspiration. They felt that the New Jerusalem was imminent. While some gnostic groups affirmed passive resistance, others became militant warriors. Some counseled civil disobedience, denounced wealth, and condemned the nobles, while others encouraged a quiet, meek, and sober demeanor. Their civil disobedience led them to poaching, pranks, outrages, and rebellions. These heretical movements first found a mass base among the poor peasants who found alien and unconsoling the Christianity imposed upon them by their lords. Much later, diffused by itinerant weavers but still within a theological framework, these movements reflected the first stirrings of a nascent nationalism that struggled against the feudal lords and the church. They were known by various names—Manichaeans, Bogomils, Cathars, Patarenes, Albigensians, and Waldensians.[6] In these and other variants, the gnostic ethos persisted and con-

[6] Norman Cohn, *The Pursuit of the Millennium* (New York: Harper & Row, 1961).

verged into the Reformation. Its advocates were imprisoned, burned at the stake, and weighted and drowned in rivers. The gnostic values ran like an underground stream, this stream disappeared as society became tranquil and stable, but in stressful times the antinomian values surfaced again and became stronger.

One of the earliest gnostic sects, the Manichaeans, devised ceremonies of preparation and initiation.[7] As an elect, they separated themselves from the worldly; they ritualized diets that would purify them and assure visions. They roamed the countryside as wanderers, beggars, and vagabond preachers. Pacifists, they repudiated killing animals. They refused to work or to comply with secular regulations and lived instead on charity. The Manichaean church, too passive and too nonresistant, was easily oppressed. Although it failed to survive the severer repression that it provoked, its name became generic for the gnostic heretical movements that recurred in the succeeding centuries.

Peter Waldo, a rich merchant of Lyon who renounced his worldly goods, was the leader of a sect, one such recurring movement, that came to be known as the Waldensians during the latter half of the twelfth century. The sect was reacting to the pressures and changes of the renaissance beginning at that time. The Waldensians were most active in northern Italy, where its sects still exist. They were an anti-intellectual mystic group, a movement of protest rather than of denial. Women as well as men were its traveling preachers. They distrusted civil authority and protested against capital punishment.[8]

[7] Steven Runciman, *The Medieval Manichee* (New York: Cambridge University Press, 1947).

[8] Sometimes these sectarian movements continue outside the establishment. At other times they are co-opted and assimilated into the system as the Franciscans were proffered as an alternative to the Waldensians or as the Peace Corps was offered to students in the decade past as an institutional alternative of dropping out and serving the people. The values and roles affirmed by the Waldensians recur among the Franciscans, the Catharists, the Beguines, and Beghards. Sometimes, as in the Reformation, they are victorious. A history of more than a

The desire to bring life closer to religious ideals rises throughout Europe at this time as people reach for a personal and more intense religious experience. Catharism, a name for the "purified," had its roots in eleventh-century Orleans and Cologne as these cities sought to wrest autonomy for themselves and to control the castles that threatened their trade routes. These sectarian values, denounced by the Church, reaffirm earlier Manichaean doctrines, and the extermination of their heresy ended with the establishment of the Inquisition, made France the greatest power in Europe, and maintained the hegemony of the Church until Luther's successful challenge. They held that matter is evil and that the world had been created by a fallen spirit. The devil was author of the visible world as God was the creator of the spiritual one. Procreation was evil, served only to permit the world to persist and to delay the return to God. The perfect believer renounced marriage and ate no food of animal origin. The Catharist belief that marriage was worse than fornication was a double-edged belief; it led the elect to celibacy, but it also sanctioned promiscuity as an expression of contempt for matter and as a way of expediting release from it. Women could be accepted as members of the "perfect" and achieved a higher status in the Cathar church than they could achieve in the Catholic.

It is difficult to ascertain the degree to which reproaches and accusations leveled against these sects were libelous myths or truthful reports. There are recurring stories that sectarians kill babies for ritual use. The Montanists were accused of cutting the throats of children, and the Circumcellians, a Donatist sect, have been charged with brutal violence, blinding and murdering opponents in the name of the Holy Spirit and begging for

---

thousand years of themes and issues rise and fall, and some are finally legitimated in the ecumenical councils of the last decade. The worker-priests today and the movement around the Berrigan brothers suggest that the legitimacy of some issues have to be rewon again.

martyrdom for themselves. This latter group professed celibacy and continence but brought along with them unmarried women during their wandering. Are these contradictions an expression of the ambivalent nature of the underlying behavior, or do they represent the libelous projections of the host community? Our own contemporary experience would suggest that both factors are present.

The Catharists affirmed a cult of simplicity in their reaction against the worldliness of medieval churchmen. It is in the context of the reawakening of Europe and the expansionism of the Crusades that one finds also the call to renew monastic ideals and ancient apostolic ways. The Beguines and the Beghards exemplify one of these waves of religious excitement that both challenges the established order or argues for submission to it.[9]

Like Peter Waldo and the Franciscans, the Beguines voluntarily affirmed poverty and renounced their patrimony for the sake of an evangelical ideal. At the same time, this movement reflects and identifies the new forces stirring in the revival of towns and cities. Their chastity and continence echoes the protest of the poor against the rich. Yet it is in precisely those circles which benefited most from material riches and affluence that one finds the recruits for the mystical excitement and renunciation.

In some regions, especially in England, the Beghards were also known as Lollards—from the word "lollen," to mutter and babble at prayers while working. The Lollards were workmen who lived communally, took vows of poverty, and usually lived as groups of unmarried men. They protested against tithes, fees, and the landed church and imitated Christ. As local power was increasingly threatened, overwhelmed and displaced by greater

[9] Ernest W. McDonnell, *Beguines and Beghards* (New Brunswick, N.J.: Rutgers University Press, 1954).

and more extensive systems of power, this rising middle class of merchants and burgesses found in John Wycliff (1395 A.D.) an organizer and spokesman for the Lollard tendencies.[10]

The Lollards maintained that temporal possessions drove out faith, hope, and charity and ruined the church and that monasteries lead only to corruption. They repudiated rituals and prayers as magic and idolatry and saw all wars as a violation of the principles of the New Testament, serving only to win through plunder and murder, glory for kings. Their focus was on the self, rather than any external authority.

This movement was popular through the fourteenth century. It was a troubled time: The Ottoman Turks advanced in the Balkans and inflicted grave defeats on the crusading armies sent against them. It was a period of disunity. The church was divided between two rival popes, each denouncing the other as heretic, and this contributed to the increasing disorientation.

The Brethren of the Free Spirit, and later the Ranters in Cromwell's time, asserted a perfectionism, free of sin, that echoed the Albigensians and made it incumbent on them to do what is commonly forbidden. They rejected chastity for promiscuity as an assertion of spiritual emancipation and self-exaltation. It was in D. H. Lawrence's phrase, more of "sex in the head" than the release of a carefree sensuality, an evangelism of free love that, like the contemporary sexual freedom leagues, seemed to be driven and compulsive.

The fifteenth and sixteenth centuries saw power shift from the Catholic South to the Protestant North, from the Mediterranean basin to Holland, Switzerland, England, and the Baltic cities. Europe was upside down.[11] In the new cities, power moved to

[10] G. M. Trevelyan, *England in the Age of Wycliffe* (New York: Harper & Row, 1963).

[11] H. R. Trevor-Roper, *The Crisis of the Seventeenth Century: Religion, The Reformation, and Social Change* (New York: Harper & Row, 1968).

new classes. Concepts of space changed as new continents were "discovered." Established rituals, experienced as increasingly empty, were repudiated; primitive Chritianity, private devotion, and inner states of piety opposed the mechanical devotion of the established church. With the dissolution of a unified Christianity, secularism grew. The monasteries acted as a barrier to the demand for new kinds of production and commerce. Heretical movements developed, ranging from Luther and Calvin on the right, who sought to institutionalize new modes and to contain the chaos, to such groups as Anabaptists and witches, who were destroyed by inquisition and terror and driven into powerless isolation.

The Anabaptist sects of the Peasant Wars in Luther's Germany[12] asserted similar values, roles, and personality styles as they rejected the "Establishment" and fought the overorganization of the church. Runciman asserts that in all gnostic movements the goal is to destroy, repudiate, and reject rather than to atone, redeem, and heal.[13] The established order is always construed as an order of evil that ought to be outraged, violated, and met with mocking self-indulgence and contempt. Membership in the cults is achieved by insight and by initiation. It requires separation from the world by a journey or by a drug. One follows the leader, the spiritual guide, or the elect, and is granted membership in a spiritual aristocracy.

Born three years after Columbus's voyage to the New World, Melchior Hoffman grew up a spiritualist and a mystic. He became an itinerant evangelist and prophet who broke away from Luther to become a leader in the Radical Reformation. He antagonized the established clergy and was driven from city after city as a seditionist. In 1533 he saw the coming of the Lord and the inauguration of the reign of saints. From his grated

[12] George H. Williams, *The Radical Reformation* (Philadelphia: Westminster Press, 1962).
[13] Steven Runciman, *The Medieval Manichee* (New York: Cambridge University Press, 1947).

prison window in Strassburg, he cried across the moat that all the apocalyptic plagues had been fulfilled, save the vengeance of the seventh Angel. Babylon was falling and they were on the threshold of the new kingdom of righteousness and peace.[14] "Redeem the time" was the Anabaptists' call. And like an echo across the centuries, Bobby Seale answers "Seize the Time,"[15] and Eldridge Cleaver, in justifying the arrest of Timothy Leary in the revolutionary "bust" of January 9, 1971, explains, "It makes me sad to do this. . . . I don't like being a jailer, but we cannot afford to jeopardize our work toward revolution in Babylon."[16]

When rituals atrophy and empty of power, there is no elect and no spiritual aristocracy other than the Establishment and its hierarchy. Disaffected individuals again find self-confirmation and recover a source of meaning in new rites of initiation and a new sense of membership. A new revelation, or a new "trip," creates a new elect and offers to marginal and declassed people a vehicle for both mobility and esteem.

The woodcuts of Lucas Cranach reflect this aversion for an academic and ecclesiastic establishment in Luther's sixteenth-century world. The illustrations show the cross on the way to heaven while the scholars are on the way to hell. They speak for spirit against the letter of the law, for grace against works. Students attack churches and universities, reject priestly vestments and university insignia and demand a common priesthood of all burghers and believers.

The Poor Conrads were a late medieval movement. With put-ons, pranks, and poaching, they fought authority; they challenged new taxes in trial by ordeal by throwing weights and measures into the river. If these stones were just, they main-

[14] E. B. Bax, *Rise and Fall of the Anabaptists* (New York: Macmillan, 1903), p. 108.

[15] Bobby Seale, *Seize the Time* (New York: Random House, 1970).

[16] Eldridge Cleaver, *Good Times* (a weekly newspaper), 10:5 (Feb. 5, 1971).

tained, God would permit them to float. In that same age of Columbus and his explorations, the Poor Conrads called for a return to feudal custom and biblical justice. They were part of the movement gathering around Luther and the Peasant Wars of 1524–1525. Astrologers noted that in February 1524 the planets would meet in the sign of the Fish. This was read as prophecy that floods would engulf the world and recalls our contemporary fantasies about collision of worlds, tidal waves, and the earthquakes predicted for the late 1960s when many in the counterculture fled eastward or took to the hills as they waited for California to sink into the sea.

The antinomians are pilgrims between the dying world and the world not yet born. In the interstices distinctions become blurred and vague, and people grope from the profane to the sacred, from the blasphemous to the austere. There is a diminution of the ego as the individual struggles and flees from the objective world and engages in a dialogue with his double, true self. His is the inflated consciousness characterized by Jung:

> Always egocentric and conscious of nothing but its own presence. It is incapable of learning from the past, incapable of understanding contemporary events, and incapable of drawing right conclusions about the future. It is hypnotized by itself and therefore cannot be argued with. It inevitably dooms itself to calamities that must strike it dead. Paradoxically enough, inflation is a regression of consciousness into unconsciousness.[17]

Nostalgic while the problems of adjustment in ambiguous situations confront him and uncertain in new roles, the antinomian invokes, as Novalis did, a magic idealism which as a romantic manifesto proclaims the antithesis between intellect and "life."[18]

[17] Carl Jung, *Psychology and Alchemy* (London: Pantheon Books, 1954), p. 461.

[18] Novalis proffered magic idealism to overcome fragmented and specialized activity and to achieve through fusion that bridging of a world

Romanticism as a Secular Variant

Generations of "flower children," the "innocent," the "guileless," the "pure in heart," who do not speak with the forked tongues of the adult world and its Establishment, recur in ages of transition and anxiety. Burned at the stake by the Dominicans and impaled on Turkish swords, the gnostic movement returns in new cults with new names. The underground stream rises in occult rites and Kabbalah, in witchcraft, and in its secular form as a romantic movement. The cry of "alienation," reintroduced by the existentialists, has been a signature of the past decade. Before its current use, Karl Marx spoke of the alienation of man from his work. The theme characteristically recurs in ages of anxiety as a referent for the loss of what is deemed sacred,[19] the sense that man is profaned, spectator and actor as two separate dissociated masks with no tie between them. Such a dissociation between the observing and the acting self

---

become too discrete. He sought a mythic homeland, which he seemed sometimes to suggest he could also find in unselving and in death.

The German Romantic, Schlegel called for a programming of happenings and of deliberately contrived illusions and fantasies which would change the commonplace into the mysterious, the vulgar into the lofty, the familiar into the fascinating, and that would make the sublime the stuff of daily life.

Madame de Stael, introducing German Romantic literature into France in 1800, emphasized the revival of medieval and Christian qualities in that movement. She celebrated the full and open heart as opposed to the "aridity" of the rationalism and agnosticism of the eighteenth century. The French word "*esprit*," Hegel remarks, invokes notions of intellect and wit. French has no equivalent for the German word "Geist," which connotes interiority, soul, and essence.

19 "All sacred things must have their place . . . being in their place is what makes them sacred, for, if they were taken out of their place, even in thought, the entire order of the Universe would be destroyed. Sacred objects therefore contribute to the maintenance of order in the Universe by occupying places allocated to them." Claude Levi-Strauss, *The Savage Mind* (Chicago: University of Chicago Press, 1967), p. 10.

induces passivity and apathy, and the word "alienation" condenses the experience of the loss of connection as one impotently confronts overwhelming power and indifferent authority. Unable effectively to determine and control one's destiny or to induce from one's environment a satisfactory response, one reacts with inertia or with hyperactivity as one surrenders to "fate."

The romantic movement became dominant in the first half of the nineteenth century. For some decades before the turn of the century, a reaction to the Enlightenment and a rejection of its values were already manifest. Romanticism was a response and an accommodation to the transition and social crisis brought about by the industrial revolution, the French Revolution, and the Napoleonic wars. The word "romantic" finds its source among the troubadours who, in an Aesopean language, spoke of Cathar and Albigensian heresies rather than the erotic, and the word bound the earlier gnostic groups and the new secular coteries. As a movement it was an adaptive response to the critical conditions in which it develops and was susceptible to the pathologies and excesses of the antinomian mode. If the orderly and the reasonable too often deteriorate into the dull, the shallow, and the complacent, the romantic repudiation often turns into silliness, indulgence, mocking extravagance, outrage, and the loss of standards.

In the romantic movement, as in the gnostic, truth was achieved through vision rather than "dry" analysis, rationality, and calculation. The intense part was valued more than the ordered whole; the central focus was on emotion, imagination, and vision. "The heart," said Pascal, "has its reasons that the Reason does not know." Common sense appeared trivial and banal and only through the act and the deed could one wrest significance and redeem meaning. Freedom and the gratuitous act were preferred to convention, balance, and restraint. Dostoevsky in *Crime and Punishment* and Gide in *Lacfadio's Adventure* both call for the gratuitous unmotivated act as a demonstration of autonomy and self-actualization. These are, it seems to me, overcompensating activities in response to a sense of helplessness and dread. The romantic trusted his own feelings rather than rules; peak experiences of vision, choice, gesture, and action alone can overcome dullness. Such experiences and acts contained their own justification, independent of their consequences.

Sensibility and insensibility, as de Sade noted, are close to one another. The romantic craved sensation, made a cult of awareness, and honed his appetite for the exotic and the macabre. He sought emotion for emotion's sake, explored the extravagant, experimented with obscure and violent feelings, and found special truths in madness and in polymorphous perversions.[20] As a scholar of the period remarked, the romantic, spiritual, or physical tourist sought periods and places that are extraordinary and exotic, where habits were likely to be strange or horrible and motives, passionate and unusual.[21] The romantic reasserted the primacy of intuitive, emotional, and inspirational values. He renewed the quest for that fusion, enthusiasm, and ''organic'' unity of which he had been deprived by Newton's image of the universe.

Just as Huizinga remarked on the compulsive weeping in the waning Middle Ages,[22] so Taine in his record of the *ancien regime* describes new fashions of weeping, swooning, and enthusiasm as characteristic behavior.[23] Groundless nostalgia becomes a central motif. Faced with the industrial revolution and with

[20] Consider in this context the existential, phenomenologic antipsychiatry of R. D. Laing, *The Politics of Experience* (New York: Pantheon, 1967). See also: *R. D. Laing and Anti-Psychiatry,* Robert Boyers and Robert Orrill, eds. (New York: Harper & Row, 1971).

[21] G. S. R. Kitson Clark, "The Romantic Element, 1830–1850," in *Studies in Social History,* J. H. Plumb, ed. (Toronto: Longmans, Greene, 1956).

[22] J. Huizinga, *The Waning of the Middle Ages* (London: Arnold, 1937).

[23] Hippolyte Taine, *The Ancient Regime,* John Surand, tr. (New York: Smith, 1931).

Blake's "Satanic mills," a zeal for folk art and for simple rural Arcadian values is reaffirmed. The Enlightenment asserted the primacy of reason and the universality of natural law; it optimistically assumed an inherent progress as it construed a mechanistic universe. The romantics denied and rejected such assumptions.

Changes from a classic to a romantic orientation are not merely matters of changing taste. Wolfflin, for example, in his *Principles of Art History*, notes the recurrence of the classical and the romantic, but seems to make them merely formal issues.[24] But to assume that these are merely stylistic changes is shallow. Such a view fails to recognize that changes are adaptive and functional; they reassert values as to the nature of man, of society, and of the universe and involve a change in orientation intended to master experience and to enable men to cope with loss, crisis, and stress.

During the Enlightenment, order, regularity, rules, etiquette, style, and ceremony were central values. A world seen as orderly and meaningful finds its rituals and ceremonies viable, its discipline appropriate, and the legitimacy of the disciplining agents established and acknowledged. The need for conformity seems to be self-evident and in the "nature" of things. Decorum and decency are deemed appropriate. Such is a classical world. It may be relevant to our purposes to note that propriety and proprium, as a referent to the self, or to *amour-propre*, share a common root.

But the antinomian, whether gnostic, romantic, or contemporary hippie, lives in a habitat of forms and rituals that have been depleted of value and meaning. He finds forms exhausted or banal. When he permits himself an emotional statement, it often is either ecstatically ineffable or "camp"

[24] Heinrich Wolfflin, *Principles of Art History* (New York: Dover, 1932).

and mocking of all sentiment as sententious. Man is the measure, but the deranged self becomes an unreliable gauge, and perception is construed as hyperbole.

If the Enlightenment valued clarity, rationality, and order, the romantics sought the allusive and the synesthetic,[25] the intuitive, and the passionate. The Enlightenment confirmed the social man, but the ideal of the romantics was the isolated wanderer, the lone melancholy rebel. If the Enlightenment embellished thought with ceremony and activity with ritual, the romantics opposed rules and regulations. If the Enlightenment asserted the primacy of the group and the civility of life, the romantics repudiated the mediocrity of the herd and affirmed the impulsive, the spontaneous, and the novel. They chose the irrational, the mystic, and the ecstatic, which they contrasted with an arid, abstract, and analytic intellectualism.[26] Romanticism opposed the mechanistic universe with a supernatural world of visions; against consciousness and rationality, it lauded

[25] Referring to synesthetic imagery in the course of a comment on Baudelaire, Adorno maintains that it fulfills a specific function. "By clouding the division between different realms of sense perception, they simultaneously try to efface the rigid classification of different kinds of objects, as it is brought about under the practical requirements of industrial civilization. They rebel against reification." Theo W. Adorno et al, *The Authoritarian Personality* (New York: Harper & Row, 1950), p. 746. But Adorno fails to appreciate that also involved in the synesthetic and the syncretistic is the need to blur the differentiation between subject and object and that the need for fusion and for ego inflation is also a motive.

[26] Wordsworth spoke of "that false secondary power by which we multiply distinctions." William Wordsworth, *The Prelude or Growth of a Poet's Mind,* text of 1805, E. De Selincourt, ed. (London: Oxford University Press, 1933), Book II, p. 26. And Coleridge said, "Self-consciousness is not a kind of being, but a kind of knowing and that too the highest and furthest that exists for us." He also spoke of "the sacred power of self-intuition." Samuel Taylor Coleridge, *Biographia Literaria* (New York: Holt and Williams, 1872), Thesis X, pp. 361–362. And Blake contemptuous of self-control, said, "Those who restrain desire, do so because theirs is weak enough to be restrained; . . ." William Blake, *The Marriage of Heaven and Hell* (London: Chatto and Windus, 1911), p. 49.

the virtues of the unconscious and the bizarre. The romantic self, alienated by and in recoil from a mechanical paradigm, saw nature instead as a benign mother or as a dark, threatening, chaotic witch. In their dreams the romantics took "trips" to Xanadu or imagined the life of the red Indian in the forests of North America before he had known the white man. If they could not find a golden age in the past or the future, they built ivory towers to escape the drab actuality of steaming factories and city slums.

It has been argued that German, French, and English romanticism had different goals, the first reactionary and conservative, and the latter two progressive and liberal. Despite their disparate goals, what binds them into a common movement is the identical commitment to enthusiasm, intuition, and irrationality and the preference for extremist solutions as adaptive behavior. With the attrition of traditional values of the nature of society and the universe, with the collapse of customary social and psychological assumptions, the antinomian maneuver recurs. It is the identity of style and of response that makes for the commonality of the variant forms of the romantic movement, that links the earlier gnostics with the contemporary hippies.[27]

It is noteworthy, too, that for Wordsworth, Blake, and their contemporaries a central motive was their disappointment with and revulsion against the French Revolution. Today's drug scene can also be understood in part as a recoil from and repudiation

[27] Among the contemporary hippies it is necessary to note role differentiations, too. As a social movement it absorbs ambulatory schizophrenics who in an earlier time might have been "hoboes" or eccentrics; young adolescent experimenters with roles; and a range of role commitments, all antinomian, from those who assert values of gurus and mystics like Alan Watts and Timothy Leary, of shamanism and Indian tribalism like Allen Ginsberg and Gary Snyder, to Merry Pranksters whose aim is *epater le bourgeois* like Ken Kesey, self-conscious Albigensians like the Diggers, hooligans like the Hell's Angels, homosexuals, Bohemians, and bored middle-class sensation tasters.

of politics, as a consequence of disillusionment with the Russian and Chinese revolutions, and the rejection of the rational, secular values these revolutions affirmed. The "egg head" is discredited not only by the Philistines, but also by the visionaries of Bohemia.

The older antinomians—the gnostics, the anabaptists, and the romantics—sought ways to outrage and provoke the Establishment. Uncouth behavior becomes a way of saying "no" to the system, of separating oneself from Philistines and "squares" by bizarre and extravagant costumes and by strange hairdresses and beards. Gautier, in the period between the Revolution of 1848 and the Paris Commune, paraded in a red waistcoat, and "Pope" Enfantin masqueraded in splendid costumes. In Germany, Father Jahn, bearded, dressed in leather, carrying staff and guitar, gathered youthful disciples who burned books and practiced physical and spiritual exercises.[28] Were those costumes used to achieve distance from the world of factory and finance and to provoke the Philistines, or was the masquerade a maneuver to demonstrate that the isolation in which these career-hungry intellectuals lived was intentional and really brought about by themselves?

Les Bouzingos

By 1830 the French vision of liberty, equality, and fraternity had been overwhelmed by the material values of the new and powerful middle class. It was a time, Musset says, in *Confession d'un enfant du siècle* when people suffered "the twin injuries of the heart: all that had been no longer was, all that would be was not yet." The Revolution of 1830 left behind it disillusion and despair. In art, politics, manners, and morals there was a

[28] Peter Viereck, *Metapolitics, the Roots of the Nazi Mind* (New York: Capricorn, 1961).

repudiation and revolt against all convention. The people had exchanged the tyranny of caste for the tyranny of money. The younger generation, confronted with the betrayal of its ideals, rejected the new establishment and turned to sex, drugs, religion, and the cultivation of the exotic and the eccentric. They explored the occult, and in outrageous and provocative speech and play, they provoked the philistine society.

Enid Starkie, writing of that time, says:

> These young people were what might be called the war generation—those who had reached adult life at the time of the July Revolution. They had been born and spent their childhood during the worst years of the Napoleonic Wars, in an atmosphere of impending doom, in the midst of increasing bad news—lost battles and military disasters. Their parents were weary of war, disgusted with tyranny, and despairing of the future, and the children inherited the restlessness and spleen of their elders so that when they reached maturity they developed a passionate desire to destroy everything and to leave no vestige of the past. They felt that before anything could be rebuilt everything must first be destroyed. . . . Their fathers had worked too hard and fought too long for the sons to care about earning a living and they thought only of stifling the voice of reason. Frivolity and eccentricity, a bacchanalia in the streets that involved rich and poor so that there was at that time as in all ages of stress an enthusiasm for dancing.[29]

The time was 1832. From March to November cholera swept through Paris and there were 20,000 victims. While the cholera raged and opposition to the new regime increased, people thronged into the dance halls. The Galope Infernal became the

[29] Enid Starkie, *Petrus Borel* (New York: New Directions, 1954), p. 49.

most popular dance. Enid Starkie quotes a German visitor to Paris in the 1830s who described the dance, "Rhythm of the music gains in speed, the gestures of the dancers become more passionate, urgent and insistent, voluptuous, rhythmic, frenetic, like the witch's Sabbath." The cancan, at that time less innocent than the music-hall version we know, despite its obscenity and lasciviousness, was more acceptable to the police than more dangerous forms of insubordination.

Auguste Viatte, traces the occult sources of romanticism that characterized that time:

> The inspired ones of 1820 and especially 1830 will give themselves over to the debauche of a frenzied anarchy and will refuse to follow any other laws than those of Nature. Their clamors, their agitation, will grieve the idealists and appear as the most evident symptom of the decomposition of the world. They will give shudders to the unwilling spectators of this new "barbarian invasion"; they will disconcert the melancholic children of the century; their howling mob will precipitate the crisis in which, around 1830, the beliefs of so many desperate people foundered.[30]

The hippies of that day were known as *les Bouzingos.* The word means "noisy, undisciplined, and extravagant," and was an epithet this group proudly wore, as they pledged with their obscene songs to fight the philistines. They saw themselves as a camp of Tartars and used skulls as drinking vessels and danced wildly and nakedly in the streets or sat naked in their gardens to outrage the neighborhood. Gerard de Nerval said, as he drank from a skull, that it was his father's. This group cultivated a black humor similar to our contemporaray underground press and they were obsessed with sadism, rape, satanism and werewolves.

[30] August Viatte, *Les Sources Occultes du Romantisme,* Vol. II (Paris: Librarie Ancienne, 1928), p. 271.

Gautier, in his *History of Romanticism*, describes these men with their hair brushed up from the sides into a high peak to simulate the flame of genius. In place of a waistcoat, some wore black velvet, tightly fitting doublets and loose jackets with wide velvet lapels, and black flowing ties. Others dressed like Spanish grandees, in Cossack boots, or in bright blue frock coats with gold buttons like those worn by an Indian Maharaja. Still others wore sweeping light blue coats lined with pale pink and fastened by pearl buttons as large as our half dollar. The leader of the group, the poet Petrus Borel, wore a red waistcoat, "the color of Polish blood," and a wide-brimmed hat with varicolored ribbons flowing down to his waist. Gautier wore a red velvet doublet and pale green trousers with black velvet stripes down the side seams.

They played at dandyism, nudism, Satanism; they used drugs such as stramonium, belladonna, and atropine to dilate their pupils and to achieve a look of strange fixity. They assumed roles either of intense passion or of impassivity and detached coolness.[31] One can only imagine the outrage of the new, earnest, money-makers and manufacturers on their way to the counting house, and their despair at their sons' behavior.

This period can stand as a prototype for a recurrent pattern of the antinomian style. Had I not located the behavior and the costumes in the 1830s, you might have assumed I was describing

[31] There was a striking change in the relations between the sexes and in women's view of their roles. A new religion, the Evadinistes (combined the names of Adam and Eve) carried the banner of women's liberation and of unisex. Sex and sensuality were exalted and whores were viewed as the apostles and the martyrs of the new religion. New styles of passionate love were affirmed and spiritual worship from afar was denounced. Women wore corduroy trousers, smoked cigars and pipes, and drank heavily. They professed to despise all decency and cultivated vice, debauchery, every kind of intoxication, and reached for all manner of artificial paradises. They revelled in horror. De Sade was their favorite reading, and they cultivated a literature of the morgue.

Haight-Ashbury or the East Village. Today the young dress in the colorful costumes reminiscent of popular myths of their childhood television-viewing. Rock and roll reaches for the same goals of the Galope Infernal of 1830. Ken Kesey organizes his merry pranksters to outrage the philistines just as Petrus Borel did. A popular song claims that kicks are getting harder to find. In reaching for kicks this generation has turned to the traditional devices of the occult and the exotic, of polymorphous perversity, as well as to the use of hallucinogenic drugs.

Baudelaire, at the beginning of the thirty-third of his Little Poems in Prose, might be speaking for today's youth: "One must always be drunk. That's the only question. In order not to feel the horrible weight of time which breaks your shoulders and presses you to the ground, it is necessary to intoxicate oneself without any letup. But how? With wine, with poetry, or with virtue, as you like. But intoxicate yourself. . . ."[32]

The Wandervogel—Communes and Tribalism

There are now an estimated 1000 rural hippie communes and at least twice that many urban communes in North America. Many of these experiment with new forms of the extended and nonnuclear family and whether they elect heterosexual, bisexual, or homosexual roles, whether celibate and ascetic or libertine, they echo earlier antinomian life styles.

These isolated young people, the cross-country hitchhikers and wandering students in search of roles, claim a tribalism that recalls a pre-World War I, German youth movement, the *Wandervogel.* They too sought the whole man, banded together and improvised rituals, sought a vigorous life and blood brotherhood, and set out upon a trip, a quest. Now, as then, young people seek to renew in folk culture, folk music, and crafts, the sense of the

[32] Charles Baudelaire, *Little Poems in Prose* (London: London Editions Poetry, 1946).

tribe. The *Wandervogel* found their anchorage in a pantheistic union with nature. In a deranged world, the search for meaning and purpose reinstates the first god—the tribe.

The greatest happening in the movement was a carnival-like event that reminds us of the Woodstock Nation or the Berkeley People's Park parade: the Meissner Fest, a celebration on Mt. Meissner, in October 1913. The movement confronted the public as a united group and in the Meissner formulation made known its desires to seek out "inner truth."[33] Some sought a mass migration movement out of the cities or to the Orient, while others sought a "secession of all those of good will" to begin building an ideal "natural" life of farming and craft settlements.

Like contemporary mimes and guerrilla theater, players toured the countryside, presenting both popular and mystery plays. These groups sought, as the "new theater" does today, to break out of the proscenium and to create a unity between players and audience. First the youth movement had called for "the convalescence of nature" to overcome the sickness of civilization. Later, a large part of the prewar *Wandervogel* ultimately turned to political action, "overcoming the error of the first stage of the youth movement: individualism. . . ." Youth culture, the leaders now said, was the blabbering of sick souls; they demanded youth power. Thus the romantic symbols ultimately were transformed into soldierly rites of falling in and marching, and the prewar guitar was replaced by flute and drum.[34]

One may also compare the hippie culture with the dadaist

[33] "German Youth stands at a historical turning-point. Youth, heretofore excluded from the public affairs of the nation and assigned to a passive role of learning . . . only an appendage of the older generation, is beginning to become conscious of itself. It is striving, independently of the tired customs of the older generation and of the commandments of a repugnant convention to shape its own life. . . ." It expressed a "nostalgia for nostalgia" as it reached for a mystic community. Werner Helwig, *Die Blaue Blume der Wandervogel* (Gütersloh S. Mohn, 1960).

[34] Luise Fick, *Die Deutsche Jugend-Bewegung* (Eugen Diederich Verlag, Jena 1939).

and surrealist movements that were a response to World War I.[35] Dada was a no-saying to the establishment. Through dreams, hallucinations, and subjection to chance, dadaists and surrealists sought a renewal of experience and vision, an antidote to the increasing sterility of industrial and mercantile life. The hippie movement is a large-scale, mass-produced, marketable version of these earlier avant-garde movements. The surrealists, however, did not opt for the flight from thought, rationality, and intellectualism as have the enthusiasts of the past decade.

The Present Situation

Today's antinomian movement repudiates rational cognition for an intuitive, visionary gnosis. Repudiating concrete, sequential thinking, a generation of university students has given credence to astrology, the I Ching, the folklore of extrasensory perception, and flying saucers and space people. Why do they retreat from rationality? What are we to make of the enthusiasm for organic foods and macrobiotic diets? Is it not, over and beyond the problem of contaminants, an expression of that ancient dualism that differentiates the spiritual pure from the material impure, the divine from the corrupt? In youth groups

[35] The Surrealists were precursors in their desire to explore consciousness, Dada in anti-rationalism, provocation and the apotheosis of youth. The Yippie style is the direct heir of the Dada movement. Before Leary, Dada advocated "blowing people's minds" and urged them to "drop out." Its members hoped by anarchistic acts of symbolic destruction to give the final coup to a dying order. Their scandals and provocations were intended to demoralize the bourgeoisie by creating disorder and emphasizing the absurdity and meaninglessness of collective values. Dada, committed only to negation, was anti-rational and anti-systematic in principle. The Surrealists, led by Breton, were not committed to disorder but were instead interested in the "irrational" unconscious aspects of experience as a source of a new, more embracing rationality. See Hans Richter, *Dada: Art and Anti-Art* (New York: McGraw-Hill, 1965) and Andre Breton, *Manifestoes of Surrealism* (Ann Arbor: University of Michigan Press, 1969).

and communes, people seek the "real self" in their return to purity, nature, and innocence. As they gather glass, paper, and tin and return these to the cycle of nature, are they paralleling the gnostic desire to gather and return to the divine its alienated fragments?

If sixteenth-century heretical groups justified the inner man and his private relation with God, they also provided him with a public framework that confirmed his identity and his membership. Likewise, in contemporary therapeutic forums, synthetic weekend communities for confession, and reports of inner or sexual, often group activity, one discerns the old Manichaean ruminations: Was it real? Am I truly of the elect? Have I found the authentic inner vision?

Today's generation has abdicated. They claim they are holding onto their own integrity and exploring their own inner experience and saying, "Count me out. I won't play the games of corporate power and gas ovens and napalm." The vocabulary of "games" denies validity to what cannot be managed or mastered.

It is ironic that this nihilistic group, so shrill in its repudiation of the IBM bit and the American way, is so American in its assumption that techniques will make a new self. They really believe in culture via "great books," music through ten easy lessons, a new personality as available as a hair tint, and they seek out multichannel sound and color, stroboscopic experiments, and drugs. And for the man or the society that has everything, there now is transcendence in a sugar cube and a way to excite the "real" self as the ultimate prosthetic.

Earlier transcendent movements, in reaching for meaning and order, used either active or passive strategies. The active drug users today use speed. If their solution is passive, they turn to hallucinogens. They do not so much make their world as surrender and lapse from it. They say that they wish to reject all that which deadens and corrupts the quick and assert their need for relatedness and contact. Yet their route, despite their longing for something more satisfying, takes them to privacy, isolation, and rejection of the world. They reject the shoddy about them only to take on a new illusion and self-deception, substituting sensationalism and private visions for reality. Casting out old institutions and traditions as "games," they have no form into which they can cast their experience, and as so often happens when left to one's own private subjective devices, they lose touch and control. Their speech disintegrates into inarticulate and uncommunicable mumblings of "I mean" and "you know" and expletives of "wow" and "out of sight" as they stumble in their solipsistic traps. This self they seek, as if it were an epiphany to be revealed rather than made by man, is a reversion to an older theology, that of a "soul" separate and apart from the body and capable of a higher wisdom. But it is a secular conversion, and students have said to me, as Dwight Moody the evangelist said after his conversion, "I fell in love with the birds, and it seemed I was in love with all creation." But such conversion and love, as William James long ago knew, is hate standing on its head rather than its feet. Conversion, in religious movements or in the surrender of Alcholics Anonymous, is a tactic of resolution and reconciliation in which one attempts to master hostility, rage, and destructiveness by overcompensation and by a process of undoing, which converts the destructive wish into its opposite. For them "turning on" really means "turning off," to withdraw, to deny feelings, and to avoid fear, anger, and desire.

An earlier generation felt an identity with a community—if not their own middle class, which they often repudiated, then at least with the idealized proletarians, the Arcadian collective farm, or the high culture of Europe. This generation knows manipulation by publicity rather than by responsive public life. The pot party or "trip" is the secular chapel in which it seeks by sensate contact to find both itself and a public. But where religious communion achieves a generalized and ritualized participation, this private communion remains fragmented, isolated, and observing of itself, and so it becomes a secular unshared, caricature of communion, with neither priest nor viable collective.

There are always pockets of disorder in any society, but these are usually contained and marginal. One may always find isolated cults of astrologers, witches' covens, spiritualist circles, ascetic bands, and libertine clubs, but these isolated circles sometimes lose their marginality, break out of their deviant stigmata, and become popular and epidemic. Once more a challenged establishment confronts old heresies and enthusiasms.

Every society elects its deviants and defines its pathology. But in times of crisis and change, the pathology may find a social platform and a public role that validates its nay-saying. In new roles deviants achieve prominence and are established in modes of behavior that otherwise might be regarded as sick. Petrus Borel, the leader of the *Bouzingo,* became a solitary, isolated paranoid after the movement declined; the leader of the Tai Ping rebellion, deprived of his role as a seer, became a patient;[36] todays' guru was once the forlorn man in the back ward of the state hospital.

The new cults of sensory awareness, meditation, encounter, naked-marathon therapy, and public confession are offered as modern psychotherapies.[37] People grope, touch, and hold each

36 Sylvia Thrupp, ed. *Millennial Dreams In Action* (New York: Schocken Books, 1970).

37 The latest movies have obligatory group therapy scenes. A new growth industry of resorts and institutes schedule weekends of massage and "exploration of the here and now feelings," and they advertise techniques derived from "transcendental phenomenology" and promise to help people find ways to "break through," to more satisfying relationships, to be free, to make life more "exciting." They offer to improve communication at "the feeling level," "the gut level" and "the nitty gritty" by being "primarily experiential" in "deeper" relationships that will lead to becoming more "joyful" as one finds inner awareness, euphoria, and creativity.

other as if physical contact is necessary to reinstate their boundaries and confirm their existence and identity.

In marginal mystic groups like Subud and in established Episcopalian churches talking in tongues returns. Like early pentecostalists and Shakers, newer secular groups use excitement, movement, touch, and dance. When the wafer and other rituals have lost their potency, Dionysian rites and the orgies, which were the initial experience of communion and community, return.

Every society establishes moral holidays that structure, sanction, and institutionalize excess and release. Festivals, as Cox suggests, are socially approved occasions for the expression of feelings usually repressed or neglected.[38] Although festivals characteristically allow excess, it is always exceptional and limited. Such temporary excesses are quite different from the current practice within the drug culture of regularly being stoned, high, and ecstatic. In a normative system the festival intensifies time perception; in the antinomian, emphasis on immediacy diminishes perspective and continuity. The continuous and enduring self, attenuated by this loss of perspective, is to be reinstated by fervor, ecstasy, and continual stimulation.

Consequences of the Chiliastic Maneuver

The chiliast, the believer in the utopian millenium, sees revolution as the only creative principle of the immediate present. "The will to destroy is a creative will," said Bakunin. Those who turn nostalgically to the past or seek to respiritualize the present move through many roles from passivity to activism. When chiliastic ecstasy turns inward and gives up the conflict with the immediate world, it tends to become gentle and innocuous.

[38] Harvey Cox, *The Feast of Fools* (New York: Harper Colophon Books, 1969).

But the utopian can swing erratically between the childlike innocence and the gentleness of flower children to an idolatrous submission to the authority of church or state and the use of force in its name. Ecstasy is achieved not only by spiritual exercises and meditation but can also be attained in the black masses of witchcraft, in the black shirts of Mussolini and the storm troopers, or in the Jesus freaks ready to beat the devil.

The romantics demonstrated that the sad, melancholy, isolated rebel could also become the conspirator who took up arms. He could swing between the poles of revolution and restoration. What begins as Byronic or Promethean defiance and self-assertion can culminate in a Bonapartist ideology and the solace of the corporate state.

Adorno describes a type, which he identifies as the "Condottiere," that appears in the setting of the increased insecurity of postwar existence.[39] He is nihilistic and is convinced that chance alone matters. Out of work and rootless, he is often an adventurer, an air ace, or motor racer. These people become "born leaders of the unemployed." Captain Ernst Röhm, the tough adventurer and founder and chief of the storm troopers, who was executed by Hitler in the right-wing purge of the Nazi party in 1934, characterized himself as an *hochverrater*. There is no simple translation of this word into English. In German it implies the role of cynical operator, arch traitor, Judas Iscariot, and Iago. An equivalent in our own setting would be the speed freak "leather" homosexual or the Hell's Angel with his enthusiasm for youth, gang bang, heavy drinking and an appetite for violence and excess.

Mannheim remarks that chiliasm has always accompanied revolutionary outbursts, and when this ecstatic belief in a millennium deserts the revolutionary movement, there remains

39 Theo W. Adorno, *The Authoritarian Personality* (New York: Harper & Row, 1950), p. 763.

behind a despiritualized mass frenzy and fury.[40] Chiliasm views revolution as a value in itself rather than an unavoidable means to a rational end. An instance of such a view may be found in the acts of the Weathermen, which have led to the repudiation of violence by Bernardine Dohrn,[41] and in the assertion of the New York Panther deserters, who said in their letter to Weathermen, "Revolution is in the final analysis . . . ARMED STRUGGLE . . . revolution is VIOLENCE . . . revolution is WAR . . . revolution is BLOODSHED." (Emphasis in the original)

[40] Karl Mannheim, *Ideology and Utopia; An Introduction to the Sociology of Knowledge* (New York: Harcourt Brace Jovanovich, 1936).

[41] *Berkeley Tribe,* Feb. 12–19, 1971, reprinted from *East Village Other.* See Bernardine Dohrn, "New Morning—Changing Weather," *The Berkeley Tribe,* Dec. 18, 1970, Liberation News Service, Dec. 10, 1970.

III. Antinomianism: The Social Context

We have grown accustomed to drug abuse as endemic in lower-class and ghetto areas, and we are alarmed to see it spread into new populations. Illegal drugs are now being used by people in class, status, and age positions in which they formerly had no place. They traditionally have been an escape route of the despairing and beaten, declassed people of the ghetto. In India and Pakistan, for instance, where the use of various forms of cannabis (marijuana) for intoxicating and euphoric purposes has been institutionalized, use has declined in the middle and upper classes and is for the most part confined to the lower class. Pakistani students inform me that the middle and upper classes now reject these drugs; they consider their use declassing.

The use of drugs is culturally patterned. In the Hindu religion drugs have a sacred function and are controlled and limited by elaborate traditions. Muslims avoid drugs in their religious practices since they are forbidden to approach God while intoxicated. There are medicinal and quasimedicinal uses for marijuana in India and Pakistan based upon tradition and folklore,[1] but with urbanization and increasing education the medicinal use in these countries is declining. Even the euphoric and intoxicant uses of drugs are structured by cultural patterns, as alcohol is in this country. Their low cost and easy availability of marijuana in the natural state facilitates its adoption by the lower classes, who habitually take a few whiffs after the day's work is done, as we might have a beer or a brandy. In the same way that the exhausted and hungry peasants and laborers in the high Andes chew coco leaves, in Pakistan and India cannabis derivatives are used by fishermen, boatmen, farmers, and laborers to alleviate fatigue, depression, and hunger. They may sip a glass of bhang, a marijuana beverage, in the evening after work to achieve an illusion of well-being and to make more tolerable the strain of their daily lives. Hungry, beaten, despairing people, whether in Asia or in this country, have traditionally turned to drugs for solace, stimulation, comfort, and forgetfulness, to escape from an intolerable present and dreary future.

Opium was introduced to this country by the Chinese labor

[1] Medicinally cannabis has been used as a sedative anodyne, hypnotic, antispasmodic, and both in old medical texts and in contemporary folklore its use is recommended for tetanus, rheumatism, chorea, convulsions, diseases of cattle and as a prophylactic for intestinal worms and for footsore disease. It is a popular household remedy for gonorrhea, dysuria, asthma, and other spasmodic conditions. As a mild sedative and diuretic it gives symptomatic relief. It is placed in the cavity to relieve toothache, and folklore recommends its use to promote sexual desire. A poultice from the fresh leaves of the cannabis plant is a common remedy for conjunctivitis, swollen joints, and other inflammatory conditions. It is given to bullocks to relieve fatigue and is burned to disinfect sheep folds.

gangs who worked on the railroads. Its use then spread to gamblers on the river boats, and to jazz musicians in New Orleans whorehouses. In the 1930s a typical opium user would have been either a single, itinerant, white worker in his mid-thirties or an immigrant in the ghetto, and each new wave of immigrants in its turn contributed to the pool of drug users.

Now we are witnessing the epidemic use of drugs by a young, affluent, middle-class population. A survey conducted early in 1969 on 87 college campuses, representing a cross section of 7 million full-time American students, reported that 38 percent of the students acknowledged use of marijuana and LSD.[2] In the San Francisco Bay Area there have been reports of marijuana use as high as 75 percent in some high schools, and other reports note the use of a variety of drugs even in early elementary grades.

What are the circumstances that induce this young, affluent population to use drugs in a way hitherto limited to the despairing and exhausted? How shall we account for the fact that the panacea of the poor has become the balm of the affluent? Why has drug use become epidemic in a hitherto resistant population?

To understand an epidemic one tries to establish the places and the conditions under which the disease has risen from its endemic reservoir to take on epidemic proportion. I suggest that social, political, and psychological factors account for the emergence of a drug culture at this particular time.

The word "antinomian" designates opposition to established norms, particularly customary moral obligations; typically the word appears in a theological vocabulary,[3] and its relevance in

[2] a) *San Francisco Examiner,* January 13, 1969. *San Francisco Chronicle,* January 18, 1971, Gallup Poll, p. 1
b) Lillian S. Blackford, "Trends in Student Drug Use in San Mateo County," *California's Health,* Vol. 27, No. 5, November, 1969.

[3] Ronald A. Knox, *Enthusiasm, A Chapter in the History of Religion, with Special Reference to 17th and 18th Centuries* (Oxford: Galaxy Books, 1961).

a secular setting may not be immediately apparent. Its original use implied an interpretation of the antithesis between moral law and gospel.[4] It designated those values and behaviors that challenged ecclesiastical authority and questioned conventional moral law. Antinomianism has a long history in many settings, and to suggest that the term be transposed into a contemporary, secular setting is to emphasize the continuities between earlier times and the present.

Our predecessors formulated their orientation, values, and conduct within a theological metaphorical system of sin and salvation, good and evil, revelation, and so forth. Later, the configuration of similar values and conduct, which elaborated commitments to enthusiasm, transcendence, faith, and ardor, was expressed within a romantic metaphorical system.[5] Today our experiences and orientations are conceptualized within a technological metaphorical system. We focus, for example, upon the pharmacology of ''mind-expanding'' drugs and the presumed effects of the electronic revolution upon media and ourselves. We tend to see our problem as unique. Because we are insensitive to history and the ready assimilation of metaphor to myth, we tend to overlook the underlying correspondences between our technological metaphors and other vocabularies and metaphorical systems.

But, though the metaphors change, similar themes recur. Religious and existential issues become paramount. Young people speak of the need for fusion with all nature. Lapsed Jewish and Christian youth become dervishes, join exotic sects like the Islamic Sufi, become Hare Krishna monks with shaven pates, rediscover the literature and practices of spiritual exercises,

[4] Namely, that faith alone is sufficient justification without adherence to moral law, the legitimacy of whose sanctions is not acknowledged.

[5] Eugene N. Anderson, "German Romanticism as an Ideology of Cultural Crisis," *Journal of the History Ideas,* 2 (1941) 301–317; J. L. Talmon, *Romanticism and Revolt, Europe 1815–1848* (New York: Harcourt Brace Jovanovitch, 1967).

learn the refined distinctions of the variant forms of Yoga and Buddhism indigenous to Tibet, China, and Japan. Reaching for ecstasy and enthusiasm first in wonder drugs, they search for and are promised new and better highs as Jesus freaks or in the exercises of Tantric Yoga. They manifest a defusion of the ego and an intensified narcissism which withdraws from the world into a passive orientation, self-manipulation, and an amplification of sensory inputs and modalities that are adaptations to the experience of alienation. Such stress and themes contribute to the antinomian personality.

The Antinomian Personality

Personality is elaborated within a matrix of values. The personality type which I call "antinomian" is manifested by one whose frame of reference is threatened or has been disrupted. He suffers from a breakdown in the balance of his control and release mechanisms and from the permeability of his body boundaries. As a result, the autistic components in his perception become dominant and the range of his receptivity and response is modified. Range and response are a function of maturation and adjustment. Growing up, becoming a person with a specific identity and a sense of continuity is an elaborate and complex task. It requires an increasing discrimination and differentiation both of oneself and of people and things in the surrounding world. The behavioral scientist studies the ways in which cues from the world and stimuli in oneself are integrated to make for the experience of constancy and reliability in shifting and changing objects and surroundings (to recognize, for example, the distinction between black and white though more light may be reflected from a black piece of coal than from a white cloth in shadow). Clinical psychologists and psychiatrists are familiar with ways in which manipulation of such internal and external sources of information, their inclusion and exclusion, are managed and expressed in such pathologic conditions as manic excitement, depression, amnesias, and flight. As ways of adjusting to stress, pathologic behavior—like a radarscope—involves hypervigilance, an incoherent, inconsistent scanning of the environment. Such scanning behavior and such adaptation is not manifest only in frank disease states. It can be expressed as well by sexual activity, the use of drugs, religious exercises, fasting, and hunger as other ways of manipulating the body and its stimuli in an effort to reestablish an enduring, consistent orientation.

The antinomian fears diffusion and depersonalization. He seeks out the stimuli of touch, texture, pain, and warmth to keep contact and to overcome boredom and insensibility. He plays at throwing away what is lost to maintain the illusion of self-determination and freedom. Through "trips" to the interior, pantheistic fusion, or sadistic and masochistic ventures he attempts to demonstrate a capacity to control himself and objects and to reinstate both self and object constancy.

The sense of isolation and separation leads him to see the world as alien and detached from himself. The bridge between self as spectator and self as actor is down. There is a confusion between the self as active agent and the self as agency. The physical, the visceral, and the concrete are of greater importance than the abstract, the generalized, and the cognitive. The antinomian personality values most the immediate and the vivid, the uninhibited and the outrageous. Feeling, texture, touch, and warmth become more important than seeing and hearing. These perceptions of contact reinstate the earliest perceptions when the infant was not yet separated out from the surrounding world and was first learning what was himself and what was other than himself. As opposed to these haptic perceptions of touch, warmth, and pain, seeing and hearing are processes that deal with signals originating at a distance, separated from the self, and these perceptions help to constitute a discrete self differentiated from objects. It is significant that the use of strobe lights, of black light, the experiences of sight and sound under the influence of LSD and of marijuana are used to break down the sense of discreteness, differentiation and to reinstate the experiences of fusion and of merging. By the use of drugs and by fasting or by spiritual exercises, visual modes are manipulated and distorted so that discrete components melt and fuse.

Antinomian is to be differentiated from the sociologist's term "anomie" and the psychologist's term "anomia." Sociologists by the term "anomie" denote a condition in which people have supposedly not incorporated the norms of their society; they live without standards.[6] The term "anomia" is the psychologist's designation for the existence of such a condition within an individual. As opposed to these sociological and psychological categories which imply a deficiency state, a lack or absence of specific values or adaptive capacities, the term "antinomian" instead implies an alternative mode of adjustment rather than a deficiency condition.

The Uses of Theories of Types

There is a tendency to protest such a typological lumping together by insisting instead on the ways in which individuals differ from each other. American psychologists maintain a strong tradition which distrusts theories of types and prefers to focus on individual differences and emphasize the ways in which a characterization excludes many individuals. Such a position always notes the exception in the type and the range of variability expressed in actuality, which surrounds any ideal and abstracted construct. These psychologists prefer data which speak of traits or performance in terms of amounts rather than in terms of classes.

But this I hold to be a pseudo-issue that futilely notes the

[6] Leo Srole, "Social Integration and Certain Corollaries: An Exploratory Study," *American Sociological Review*, 21 (1956) 709–716.

obvious difference between the particulars and the generalizations that one can derive from them. True, the derivation of an arithmetic mean or median from a distribution of numbers or events sacrifices and loses specific information. But though particularity is lost, it becomes possible to describe general components of the cluster or class. It makes comparison and contextual scanning possible. Abstraction also makes analytic operations more accessible. Instead of being swamped by facts and bits, it becomes possible to contrast and compare larger amounts of information. Although individual differences persist, and people react to particular environments, behavior is organized in consistent enduring patterns which maintain their structure over time. Despite the differences between ancient Greece and seventeenth-century France, one finds in the portraits of Theophrastus and in those of Jean de la Bruyeré the same coherent configuration of traits and motives which cluster and hang together and around which character is organized. In both of those writers, as in those of the present age, one can still recognize such characteristic types as the flatterer, the boaster, the gossip, the miser, the officious or the affected man.

Such descriptions use as a framework not only traits and motives but such explanations as temperamental styles or physical elements and humors; of body types, for example, the dominance of fat, muscle, or nervous tissue; or erogenous zones, such as oral or anal personalities; and of various other clinical categories. In psychology as in literature, there has been a persistent effort to determine organizing principles that can order diverse and varying needs, motives, traits, elements, and factors into structured types.

The formation of such typologies does not require that the name or classification have a "real" organismic existence. It need not be reduced to a causal point in a nerve ending or a gene. It is enough if a typological construct integrates apparently disparate bits of information into continuities that demonstrate the interrelation of parts. Such a theoretical formulation ultimately justifies itself if it orders data meaningfully and makes it possible to predict events, to make deductions from type to component parts, and to account for variability and deviation from the type.

More than the mere accumulation of isolated facts, we are concerned with the classification of data into categories. These constructs may cut across other categorical systems. What is relevant is whether they order the data to reveal new relationships and point to characteristic ways in which people act. Such roles as pure cases represent ideal types. They, like the mean or the median, are expressions of locations or extreme points on a continuum. They are justified because they make it possible to conceptualize diversity, to reach beyond description for inferences that may help to explain the events we scrutinize, and to discover configurations previously overlooked.

Adorno, in building his case for the authoritarian personality, wrote, "People form psychological classes inasmuch as they are stamped by variegated social processes," and further maintained that the critique of typology should note that many people are not and have never been individuals.[7] They remain standardized and with little individuation. It is by now a cliché to observe, for example, that nonconformist styles in clothes and hairdress have themselves become uniforms.

Changing Times and Changing Types

Social and political events confront us with problems and provoke questions that impel psychologists to revise their constructs and research strategies. For example, the pragmatic need to identify and cope with prejudice and the fascist mentality of

[7] Theodore W. Adorno et al, *The Authoritarian Personality* (New York: Harper & Brothers, 1950), p. 744.

the 1940s led Adorno and his colleagues to conceptualize the authoritarian personality. They demonstrated that traits such as conventionality, submissiveness to authority, aggressiveness, projection, and manipulativeness appeared to be functionally interrelated. Rather than appearing as isolated traits, they interacted dynamically within a process. This investigation stimulated research for more than a decade. It focused attention on authoritarianism as an adaptive technique and as a character structure.[8]

The fact that with changing social conditions new configurations of behavior emerge and new roles are institutionalized does not necessarily imply the appearance of new traits. Such behavior may have been endemic or latent in many persons and may have required only a stimulus to become active. Instances of deviance may find social support, and behavior that formerly was an isolated characteristic can be confirmed as a role. Given the appropriate circumstances, latent structures and recessive, or marginal, behavior find socially channelled outlets. The endemic becomes epidemic.

If such behaviors persist and recur, the study of their manifestation may help to clarify determinants of the self and of roles enacted to validate one's assigned or adopted status. It should illuminate, from another view, the development and the mean-

[8] Adorno and his associates devised scales that assessed attitudes toward authority, the relationship between social and political control, and the control of one's own impulses. He separated the respondents into those who had high or low scores on these scales of attitude towards authoritarianism and impulse control. In contrast to the authoritarian low, who, despite the fact that he is antiauthoritarian, had a strong superego and whose conscience shows that he had internalized an identification with his father, Adorno noted the existence of a group he designated as the impulsive low group. These respondents, whom he identified with actors, circus roustabouts, vagrants, addicts, and prostitutes represented—despite the fact that they, too, were anti-authority—another syndrome. This group, he held, would be weaker in ego structure and in impulse control as well as deficient in super ego formation. *Ibid.* p. 776.

ing of deviance. In arguing the case for an antinomian personality, differentiated from other typological modalities, it should be clear that the construct is not annulled by variability of some of the associated elements or by differing social settings in which the construct is employed.[9]

In these differentiated categories identical traits may be included. Common traits may endure and rise in different configurations as facets of the same underlying process. Laboratory science leads to categories other than social science or clinic constructs. Yet, there may be an underlying communality, manifested consistently in different settings where the focus is on different aims that recur in typological constructs.[10] Such constructs and variables may represent partial approaches to the same ongoing functional process.

Preoccupation with the authoritarian personality has now been replaced by concern with other styles and patterns of conduct: the politics of "dropping out," the resurgence of religious interests, the psychedelic cults of "mind expansion,"

[9] Typologies are construed in differing settings to meet varying goals. Thus, typologies have been concerned with the classification of diseases, perceptual styles, temperaments, and morphological somatotypes. In medicine and psychiatry the aim is to meet problems of diagnosis, prognosis, and classification of disease and problems of institutional management. Some psychiatric typologies remain more descriptive than explanatory while others seek to link variables in a higher order inference. The fact that currently the disease model itself is under serious scrutiny and challenge does not necessarily invalidate the earlier constructs. It suggests only that the same data can be ordered in new ways, encompassing a wider range of variables to reveal new meanings and relationships.

[10] Such constructs are: color abstraction vs. form abstraction (Kulpe) color type vs. form type (Scholl), subjective type vs. objective type (Stern), syntropic type vs. idiotropic type (Wertheimer and Hesketh), extratensive vs. introversive type (Rohrschach), B-type vs. T-type and disintegrate type vs. integrate type, (Jaensch), suggestibility type vs. non-suggestibility type (Janet), field-dependent type vs. field-independent type (Witkin), low body-barrier type vs. high body-barrier type (Fisher and Cleveland), and, doubtlessly other studies.

the ideology of drug abuse, and other components of the hippie ethos. These activities, values, acts, and roles seem to comprise a unified and integrated system of conduct.

The Hippie as Antinomian

We live in an epoch of wars and revolutions. Established institutions and values crumble and are repudiated. The British Empire is at an end and America's claims to be the heir apparent are not being honored. Radicals, shaken by the Khrushchev revelations and the internecine struggles of the Russians and the Chinese, are dismayed as they see these countries devour their children. Major breakthroughs in technology and new sources of energy have introduced a new industrial revolution. Racial groups demand civil rights and disrupt customary roles and power relations. Bureaucratic governmental and corporate structures have depersonalized human relations and confront people only in "rational" functions rather than as human respondents.

In America and in Europe, as it becomes Americanized, youth lives in a society that offers no meaningful and significant institutional roles to define and structure its status as adolescents. Faced with new demands, women grow up uncertain and disenchanted, and young men, immobilized in indecision, linger in school for draft deferments rather than commitments to chosen vocations. Satiated with violence, they unblinkingly read in the news about "kill ratios," and they endure a war whose moral basis has been questioned as no other has in recent times. Protests appear ineffective. The vast bureaucratic and corporate world continues in its course, indifferent to protest and dissent.

The immediate progenitors of the current diffusion have been the ex-Harvard pundits, organized in Timothy Leary's International Foundation for Internal Freedom, the followers of Alan Watts and Aldous Huxley, and the hipster, beat, and new wave movements of the 1950s It was the decade of McCarthy, of the heating up of the cold war, of the Khrushchev revelations, of the growing knowledge of what the atomic bomb has wrought and what it threatens for the future. Once, if one joked, "Who listens?" it was a private joke about one's psychoanalyst. Today the question, "Who listens?" implies that the government is heedless and that campus officialdom is not responsive.

The post-McCarthy world discourages criticism and social protest, demands consensus, and refuses to sanction opposition. In this world inhibited protest and aggression detour to the interior self. The officialdom that censures picket lines and public protest fails to ask whether there may not be a relationship between discouraging such activities and the increased use of drugs. The epochs of the failure of nerve, of romanticism, and of god-seeking consistently follow hard upon the epochs of the lost cause. The self seeks new anchorage points, new grounds of certainty upon which it can take root.[11]

The student generation of the 1930s was a committed generation, which was neither lost nor homeless. It challenged ROTC, supported the New Deal, fought fascism, and defended the Spanish Republic; the students of the 1940s found meaning and morale in the unconditional war to destroy Hitler and

[11] Such a view appears to be supported by the recent studies in sensory deprivation which underscores the reciprocal feedback between inner and outer stimuli and the need for an optimal homeostatic relation between them. There seems to be a reciprocal relationship between the ethos of a people and its accommodation to a lost cause or a lost dream, as exemplified by ideologies of mysticism and god-seeking of romanticism, subjectivism, and expression of the self. Gilbert Murray in his "Five Stages of Greek Religion" first noted the relationship in the period following the decline of Athens, which he named "The Failure of Nerve." This stage has manifested itself periodically throughout history and seems to me clearly in evidence after 1815, 1848, 1870, 1905, 1917, and today. Buber distinguishes "epochs of habitation" and "epochs of homelessness" and suggests that in the latter, "in the ice of solitude man becomes a question to himself." *Between Man and Man* (London: Kegan Paul 1947).

Nazism and, beyond their apocalypse, dreamed of the new world to which they would come home; the betrayed youth of the 1950s became beat when they found they returned to business as usual, and the cynical young of the 1960s turned hip and cool. How does one act when one no longer trusts? Sit out the game, hedge, or play the system anyhow? And if one is not drafted, then chuck school as also phony? One defense against depersonalization is to turn from the outside to the internal milieu. If one cannot reason with the system or influence it, if one is only beating one's head against the wall, why bother to do anything except take a trip to the interior?

The unresponsive, dehumanized rationality of technological and bureaucratic systems, which take people into account only as expendable resources and the stuff of kill-ratios, leaves youth with a sense of impotence and dependency. Out of such situations comes Pascal's cry about the feeble mote, flickering in a vast and indifferent universe, and the existentialists' complaint of a world bereft of meaning and of god. The cry of the "absurd" asserts the loss of an anthropocentric cosmos and of normative myths.

We live in a time that permits the psychotic's fanciful vision of world destruction to coincide with the actuality of atomic brinkmanship, a time in which the apocalyptic vision finds reinforcement in the sudden recognition that we do, in fact, live within a shallow, fragile, delicately balanced ecological system that supports the only kind of life we can have.

Some will argue that people have always lived with the threat of early death by plague, war, or hunger. The older generation goes on about its business, accommodating to the threat and planning for the future. Why then does the younger generation live as though each day were its last? Over and above the crises and disillusionments we share, there is one additional experience that is unique, and I believe crucial, for the young. This additional factor seems to me to offer a plausible explanation for their demoralization, their turn to the cult of immediacy, and their use of hallucinogenic drugs.

Anyone born after 1945 spent his childhood in weekly, scheduled rehearsals for apocalypse, and that experience has become the central element in his selfhood. We have become so inured to napalm and kill-ratios and have learned to take terror so much for granted, that we fail to sense what the childhood of this generation was like. Do you recall the usual Friday air raid drills of fifteen or twenty years ago? Do you remember the decal pasted over the kitchen sink that read, "When the siren sounds do not use your telephone. Turn your radio to 640 or 1240," Ask your children. They remember. They remember the sirens. They remember the air raid drill at eleven o'clock every Friday. They remember that in the kindergarten and early grades they were instructed "When the siren sounds, get under your desk. Put your head between your knees. Never look out the window. It is not only the shattering glass but the searing flash you must avoid. It can blind you." They remember bringing home a note from school that asked about evacuation routes and whether their parents wished to meet them in some distant town. They remember the insane fantasies of bomb shelters and stockpiled foods, the concern about radiation and contaminated milk, the speculation as to whether the atomic-bomb testing was deranging the weather—all this was a part of the daily life. The dimensions of these experiences were and are greater for the young than for those over thirty.

I am constantly surprised when a student or patient in his early twenties begins, "Ten or twenty years from now"—and then always and inevitably adds "If I'm alive then." I'm never prepared for this, and I'm surprised every time. Is it because I'm more optimistic or more insensitive or that I suffer from a massive denial of what confronts us all? My generation has survived two world wars. Perhaps we have a historical perspective into which we have assimilated the present predicament, and thus we fail to scan it with the same urgency that younger people do. We grew up in a world that believed in a future. George Wald, professor of biology at Harvard and Nobel Laureate, in his now famous address at the Massachusetts Institute of Technology on March 4, 1969, said: "I think that what we are up against is a generation that is by no means sure that it has a future."[12] The perspectives of past and future are part of the habitat in which the person develops and grows. The belief in the inevitability of a future stabilizes behavior. The loss of a future perspective makes immersion in sensory experience a necessary adjustment.

Meanwhile, a frightened or outraged establishment seeks to control the frenzy and to prevent the desertion of its youth by a proliferation of services and techniques. They are busily setting up halfway houses, treatment clinics, or educational programs. But we are treating a symptom and failing to diagnose the underlying disease. The young see these programs only as another manipulation which asserts a set of values that they repudiate and that is intended to bring them back into the system of business-as-usual. They are totally unconvinced by the rational case which the straight and square world is trying to make for sobriety, responsibility, and health. They counter these values with an ideology of kicks, enthusiasm, and ecstasy and make being stoned and high a way of life. Except as consumers and soldiers, the young have no significant roles in work, in the community, or even in their homes. We have herded them into the pens of schoolyard and campus, and the only self-affirmation left them is to say "no" to this assignment.

Thus today's antinomian youth scorns his establishment as evil and corrupt, deplores the aimless, trivial preoccupations of family and business life, and repudiates forms and rituals he finds empty and dead.

The current antinomian style is expressed in the contemporary preoccupation with drugs as a gimmick of transcendence and as a social movement. It finds expression in the theological assertion that "God is dead," in the development of sexual freedom leagues

[12] George Wald, "Address at MIT," March 4, 1969, reprinted in *The New Yorker*, March 22, 1969, pp. 29–31.

sponsoring orgiastic communions and challenging traditional sexual roles, in the growth of homosexual communities, and in new art forms, such as the theater of the absurd, the spontaneous "happening," the drama that abandons the proscenium separating stage and audience, and all the graphic arts which reflect the diffusion and breakdown of objects and of orientation to them.

In this context one can question McLuhan's argument that the synthetic and syncretistic modes and the new tribalism can be seen as products of electronic technology which has displaced visual linear perception.[13] They can also be seen as additional evidence of antinomian fusion, which typically rejects visual perspectives and the constancy of objects.

In 1887 and 1888, long before the new electronic technology could modify perception, Nietzsche correlated nihilism with a sensibility that had become more irritable and with the exposure to intensified and disparate impressions. "The tempo of this influx prestissimo; the impressions erase each other; . . . Men unlearn spontaneous action, they merely react to stimuli from the outside."[14] Unlike McLuhan, whose focus is technological, Nietzsche described the centripetal forces leading to disintegration of the self as a factor in the encroaching nihilism. He described the loss of aim, unity, and "truth," which made the world appear valueless. He noted the sense of emptiness and the attempt to overcome it by intoxication, hedonism, enthusiasm, mysticism, and "the voluptuous enjoyment of eternal emptiness."[15] He remarked upon "the multitude and disgregation of impulses and the lack of any systematic order among them" and of the despair that follows upon the experience of being powerless against men, so that one reduces all problems to questions of pleasure and displeasure.[16]

13 Marshall McLuhan, *The Gutenberg Galaxy* (Toronto: University of Toronto Press, 1962).

14 Friedrich Nietzsche, *The Will to Power,* Walter Kaufman, ed. (New York: Random House, 1967), p. 47.

15 *Ibid,* p. 20.

16 *Ibid,* p. 28.

There is renewed interest in the Kabbalah, Tarot cards, and astrology as attempts to read one's fate in an indifferent universe. The antinomian ethos reaches beyond the obvious hip and bohemian cults. Current philosophical and scientific models in part reflect these values, whether as ideological positivism that stems from the anguish of uncertainty or in the current modishness of phenomenology as a method and philosophy. The phenomenologist is acutely aware of the diverse and protean forms of appearance. They seem to him to negate any sense of continuity, structure, or order other than that created by the self, and he beats against the walls of his solipsistic universe.

This ethos leads to the search for a "psychology of being," to the quest for peak experiences, and to the ideology of self-actualization.[17] The cultivation of idiosyncracy becomes an honored vocation. When institutions fail, when boundaries break or become permeable, when external frames of reference lose their validity, impulses and drives within the individual expand in disarray and overcome controls. The inflated individual is then compelled to find a new principle of order and control within himself. He experiments with the fragmentation of perception of objects and of self. He explores thresholds of pain, light, and sound, seeking a way out of his constant refractory phase. He seeks to bind and sustain a sense of immediacy. He embarks on a subversive program of willful, deliberate derangement in the hope that he can purge the accidental, the banal, and the trivial

[17] Self-actualization is more a new politics of despair than a psychology, whether it is sponsored by Maslow or by Norman Brown. It is a revolt against "repression," which as Marcuse noted, "promotes existence in that immediacy which, in a repressed society, is bad immediacy. It isolates the individual . . . encourages nonconformity and letting go in ways which leave the real engines of repression in the society entirely intact. The desublimation involved in this sort of self-actualization is itself repression inasmuch as it weakens the necessity and the power of the intellect." Robert Paul Wolff, Barrington Moore, Jr., and Herbert Marcuse, *A Critique of Pure Tolerance* (Boston: Beacon Press, 1965), p. 114.

and renew the world. Since external sources of identity have been discredited and their authority is no longer honored, the antinomian seeks to establish and maintain his identity by hyper-irritation of the self.

Mysticism, transcendence, "kicks," and ecstasy become dominant aims. The hippies seek a golden age to renew the lost innocence of childhood or to find the purity of the ancient apostles and the integrity of the noble savage. The turn to populism and folk ballads is an attempt to renew a national myth as one form of identity. The antinomian longs for relationship and unity and seeks to fuse himself with a group, a leader, and a cult of friendship and "love" that can overcome his uncertainty and supply him with support. In scorning corruption, in rejecting the smug, the complacent, and the unjust, he may glorify whatever he finds that gives him a sense of relatedness. He may find this in the church or in the state.

Alienation

When mobility is blocked and roles are ambiguous or discredited, when one needs to avoid fear, threat, and loss of membership, the experience of time changes. Under such conditions immediacy becomes an imperative style. Yet it is always now, and past and future are events of memory and anticipation. But it is now only if one knows how to move in and take title; instead, the depressed sulk in the basement of memory and the obsessive run to the outer margins of anticipation while the house remains vacant and unpossessed. To be alienated is to be alienated from duration, from one's own body, and from others.

The cry of alienation is embedded in a dualistic view that splits subject and object and sets the self against the other, God against the world, man against nature, and the individual against society. We shadowbox with names and categories and confuse these nouns with actual things. Plato long ago said that we never apprehended reality directly but, like men living in caves, tried to surmise reality by the shadows it cast on the walls of our caverns. Our subject-predicate language builds dualism directly into the realities that we construe and is not inevitable or in the nature of things. Other cultures and other languages construe and organize experience in different ways and slice reality into different categories. For example, where the westerner as captain of his soul announces, "I shot a deer," and sees himself as the agent bending the world to his will, the Wintoon Indian of the Sacramento Valley would say, "The deer died for me," living as he does in an environment with which he complies as part of a whole rather than one which he attempts to coerce.[18]

Consciousness, reality, and time are interrelated, and the dualistic formulations we construe are a function of our language and our derangement. Such formulations are the expression of a lost sense of community and of an extrusion from one's field so that one has to grope for "authenticity" and reach for ways to be real. When there is an interpenetration of value and fact, when norms are accepted as in "the nature of things" and "reality," such a fragmentation does not take place. Where a relative stability of facts, things, and values exists, one lives with title and membership in a community, as part of a shared public that sustains one so that it is even possible to lapse from self-involvement. The awareness of self usually returns like a nagging toothache only in moments of stress, ennui, and disequilibrium. It is only when the image reflected by the public mirror, or the "looking-glass self," as the sociologist Cooley called it, blurs and becomes diffused that immediacy, sensibility, and ongoing consciousness become imperative.

[18] Note Buber's view of this ruptured state: "Institutions are 'outside' where all sorts of aims are pursued. Where a man works, negotiates, bears influence, undertakes, concurs, organizes, conducts business, officiates. . . . Feelings are 'within' where life is lived and man recovers from institutions." Martin Buber, *I & Thou* (New York: Scribners, 1970).

In losing the sense of order, the antinomian also loses his boundaries. He asserts the primacy of the ''natural'' self and of its impulses and desires and rejects counsels of discrimination and control. Whether his behavior is due to a stimulus hunger or a hyperirritability, whether it expresses a need to augment or to avoid stimuli, the antinomian seeks the excessive and the extravagant. In self-assertion he hopes to regain lost anchorage and orientation points.

Sex roles are repudiated or diffused, ascetic and ecstatic exercises are cultivated, and libertine polymorphous perverse games become more widespread. Exhibitionism and pornography find new acceptability. The ennui and insensibility accompanying stimulus hunger or satiation overreach their refractory phase in sadism and violence. Pantheistic cosmic expansion, erotic moment, manipulations of immediacy—all are attempts to bind the self and to reinstate its boundaries. This is a rage for order.

Swingers, wife and husband swappers, gay liberation, communes with group marriages and principled promiscuity, the heightened consumerism of sex, and the expressions of sex as politics—all invoke personal rights and personal liberties when public identity and relationships lapse. Government permissiveness, for example, the modification of standards for obscenity and pornography, support this repressive desublimation, which offers nakedness and circuses and permits erotic liberties so long as these do not lead to presumptions againt property or challenges against the established order.

Astrology

Newsweek reports that astrology now has some 10 million fully committed adherents and an estimated 40 million dabblers, making this once marginal activity an epidemic.[19] Twelve hundred of the 1750 newspapers in the United States carry daily horo-

[19] *Newsweek,* "Digging the Stars," January 13, 1969, p. 54.

scopes, and almost every major women's magazine runs a monthly column. The Dell Publishing Company alone releases some thirty horoscope magazines and in 1968 sold 8 million copies of its purse-size edition. Beyond the small talk about one's natal sign lies the implication that the fault is not in ourselves but in our stars and beyond our will. If one is not master of one's fate, one can at least learn to read the signs and accommodate to the indifferent and inexorable cosmic and social process. The cosmological metaphor expresses the experienced relationship between self and society, as may the metaphorical perception of one's own body.[20]

Astrology serves to make the cosmos anthropocentric again, even while it affirms a depersonalized and merciless transcendance. It asserts the irrationality of abstract, anonymous, unapproachable authority and power. The "opaque and inscrutable" face of a highly organized and institutionalized society, experienced as unresponsive, unreasonable, and absurd, is projected into the heavens. Adorno suggests that even when interest in astrology is admittedly ironical, it functions as an ideology to justify dependence, passivity, and accommodation.[21] The individual no longer has to resolve contradictions but can view them as dichotomies to be treated serially; he no longer has to struggle to overcome obstacles but can surrender to the preordained and inevitable. Astrology's anti-intellectualism also deprecates the scientific establishment and hence discredits the most potent myths of a technological society.

Two Antinomian Modes

Passivity and activity are alternate antinomian modes. Ascetic and ecstatic, retreat and attack, quietism and aggression, passive

[20] Mary Douglas, *Natural Symbols* (New York: Pantheon, 1970).
[21] T. W. Adorno, "The Stars Down to Earth," *Amerikastudien Jahrbuch* (Heidelberg: Universitats Verlag, 1957), p. 2.

resistance and violence, control and release, discipline and pleasure—all are alternative modes for meeting stress and are a function of whether threat is seen as originating within the self or outside.

This was sharply delineated during the recent confrontation between Eldridge Cleaver and Timothy Leary.[22] In a radio address from Algiers, released on tape in the United States, Cleaver criticized Leary, repudiated "ego trips and the magic-wand approach," and deplored "substituting magic words for cold calculating confrontation with reality." The man who had written an introduction to Jerry Rubin's *Do It*[23] rejected LSD as a revolutionary instrument, demanded that the white counterculture be critically reassessed, and spoke of Rubin, Abbie Hoffman, Allen Ginsberg, and Stew Albert as "that silly psychedelic movement." Even this confrontation between the ascetic and the ecstatic parties repeats history. Several years ago the Haight-Ashbury Diggers abandoned the street scene for communes. They felt that the street had become corrupted, commercialized, and co-opted by the business world. They denounced the commercialization of rock and acid rock and called for new forms and a new ethic as they retreated to the countryside.[24]

Cleaver's view has received support from another significant and influential quarter. Herbert Marcuse, one of the most consistent mentors of the counterculture, said in an address at the

[22] Eldridge Cleaver, *Good Times, A Weekly Newspaper*, San Francisco 10:5 (February 5, 1971), pp. 8–12.

[23] Jerry Rubin, *Do It* (New York: Simon & Schuster, 1970).

[24] Cox speaks of this when he says: "to frolic and gambol in what *is* can produce as its extreme a lack of any interest in hoping, creating, or changing. To express it in the language of theology, a needed emphasis on *incarnation*, the presence of the spirit in the flesh can, if overdone, lead to a kind of presentism, a total absorption of interest in the here and now. This presentism can in turn slip over into a supine acceptance of the world as it is and the consequent disappearance of fantasy, hope, revolt, or vision. . . . It looks forward to nothing and risks satiation and boredom!" Harvey Cox, *The Feast of Fools* (New York: Harper Colophon Books, 1969).

University of California, Berkeley, "The period of beautiful spontaneity of hippie rock and shock is over. . . . The period is over because the Establishment has become immune against shock, against ego trips styled as political action."[25]

The present antinomian generation was born after 1945. It began to come of age early in the sixties. These are the people who say that kicks are getting harder to find and for whom happenings and bacchanalian block parties become the politics of abdication on the one hand, and the search for instant community on the other. Whether they adopt politics of abdication or disruption, their efforts are to intensify their present time perspective as a means of coping and of finding ground for their integration and their selfhood.

We are seeing the reaction to the civilian defense policy and the bomb drills of the 1950s. We are looking at the casualties of the cold war and our atomic policy. We cannot prevent the casualties by merely offering the techniques and services of emergency first aid.

There is some indication that, while we of the establishment are still mobilizing first-aid cadres, the young are moving beyond withdrawal and the drug scene to a new political activism and are demanding major changes in our social orientation. If we have been concerned and dismayed by their dropping-out, we seem even more concerned by their demand for participation. Given the choice, I am afraid that too many of us prefer the docile drug user to the rude political activist. We are unprepared to come out from behind protocol and procedures, to make a relationship with people who are challenging our basic values, to listen, to talk, and to change. We have failed to understand that the issue is not the Peoples' Park; it is not the Free Speech Movement or the Filthy Speech Movement; it is not even drugs.

[25] Herbert Marcuse, *5 Lectures* (Boston: Beacon Press, 1970), pp. 14–15.

The issue in each of these confrontations and in those that lie ahead is the demand for a relationship, for an unswerving allegiance to human values above those of the marketplace and the military, and for a commitment to their future. And in the end, their future is the only one we have.

Il y a un cogito du phallus. Je bande donc je suis, *et les femmes ne sont guere rassurees de ce fait. De cette absence de cogito phallique resultent des deviations, perversions,*[1]

—Jean Marie Auzias

IV. The Tuned Organism: Body Image, Sensibility and Self

In an effort to make sense of the epidemic of drug abuse of the last decade, I have suggested that this behavior can be understood as the expression of a social movement that recurs in specific and typical historical circumstances, but for the moment I am returning to an organismic framework. Social and historical events begin and end with people. Changing social conditions are associated with and articulated by changes in the coping ego and in the perceived and construed self.

[1] "There is a cogito of the phallus. I get a hard on, therefore I am, and this fact doesn't help women too much. From an absence of this phallic cogito result various deviations, perversions, . . ." Jean Marie Auzias, *Clefs Pour le Structuralism* (Paris: Seghers, 1967), p. 174.

I shall attempt to make explicit the relationship between drug abuse and the manipulation of the body image. If such a case can be made, it will build a link between endemic processes and epidemic conditions and support a psychohistorical model for the study of personality. It offers also a theoretical focus, beyond the clinical sources for my views, that may direct us to new experimental designs and hypotheses.

Such a theory would prove useful not only in clarifying an acute social problem, but in serving to establish a sounder basis for understanding addictions and perversions, both of which need a theoretical organizing principle. In the present climate of cultural and social relativism, which diffuses and dilutes all issues into matters of taste, style, modes of labeling in which all sense and meaning are swamped in a cultural nihilism, the need for such a theoretical grounding is even more imperative.

If we get past the word "psychedelic" and question the operational consequences of drug ingestion, we find an intensified awareness of the body and a shift in its focus and orientation. General feelings of conscious existence, as it is normally sensed in the functioning of the body, are either amplified or tuned down; attention shifts and there are distortions in the experience of the body and the surrounding field. Emotions appear to be separate from the individual and are expressed concretely so that metaphor and analogy are conceived as real things. Affect may be projected onto the outside world which is then literally seen animistically, for example, as angry clouds or weeping trees. The world becomes pregnant with meaning. The separated emotion leaves the self emptied and withdrawn. The encapsulated self may even be experienced as a separate entity, for example, a cloak thrown across a bed of whose ownership one is uncertain. At such times, one experiences isolation, terror, and dread.

Drugs are only one way of producing these effects. Young children and artists often have synesthetic experiences without the benefit of drugs. What Freud has characterized as the oceanic feeling, what Jung has defined as ego expansion, and what William James has pointed to as cowering dread and loathsomeness, have been states known without drugs and defined by psychologists, artists, and mystics.

Drug ingestion creates either microscopic or macroscopic distortions, and modification and modulation of visual and tactile experiences so that new figure-ground relations are established. The perception of space, time, and self become less differentiated. They regress to more global and infantile forms. The perception of time is modified so that thought speeds up and the stream of consciousness may flood or freeze. Thinking and affect become concrete and archaic, and the identification and localization of inside and outside are confused. Sensation becomes abnormal, morbid, and depraved. Paresthesias may be acute, amplified experiences of burning, prickling, and crawling on the skin, or one may experience anesthesia, a loss of sensation and feeling where one customarily expects to find it. There also occur synesthetic crossovers from one sense to another so that, for example, one sees sound as color and translates sensations from the dimension of one sense modality into another. Percepts of color, space, size, and time become deranged and intensified, and a split between percept and concept often occurs.

In describing drug experiences in such specific terms, can we not maintain that these sensory and perceptual operations are all integrated as a shift in the stability, rigidity, or lability of body image, ego, and the structure of the self? The modulation and manipulation of vestibular perception, which pertains to orientation and movement, of kinesthetic, visual, and tactile perception, and changes in the experience of warmth, pain, texture, and all senses of touch, are the specific operations of self-management.

There is an established literature on the study of the body image that provides clues for understanding drug behavior and for refining and isolating those variables which have been overlooked in drug studies. It is a classic aphorism of the psychiatric literature to say that the body image is the nucleus of the ego,[2] that, in fact, the body image is the archaic ego that persists as a perpetual, ongoing surf, the ground upon which the more differentiated self and ego are construed. The body image is the integration of all perception and affects.[3] It extends from inside the depths of the organism outwards to the limits of space and time. The literature of psychopathology holds that excessive concern and attention to the body is developmentally less mature and that it is associated with personality disorders which may be expressed as narcissism, hypochondria, delusions, fetishism, perversions, exhibitionism, mutilation, and autoscopy (the experience of being detached from and viewing one's own body, a phenomenon not unusual among schizophrenics and sometimes reported by drug users). Changes in the perception of the body image are reported as a result of psychotherapy, hypnosis, or use of alcohol and other drugs. The relation between body image and abstract thinking[4] and archaic thinking[5] have been reported.

Tattooing can also be understood as such an effort to locate and fix the boundaries of the self by marking and stimulating the body. Like a new car or hat, tattooing involves the use of an external sign as a label and confirmation of the self. It is probably not an accident that young children in our culture ink their hands and play at tattoos as a basic orientational act. Tattoos are common among soldiers, sailors, and prisoners. Do they require

[2] Sigmund Freud, *The Ego and the Id* (London: Hogarth, 1927).
[3] W. Clifford M. Scott, "Some Embryological, Neurological, Psychiatric and Psychoanalytic Implications of the Body Schemes," *International Journal of Psychoanalysis,* 29, (1948), pp. 141–155. "The Body Scheme in Psychotherapy," Brit. J. Med. Psychology, 22, (1949), pp. 139–150.
[4] Sylvan Keiser, "Disturbances in Abstract Thinking and Body Image Formation," *Journal of the American Psychoanalytical Association,* 6 (1958), pp. 628–652.
[5] Andrew Peto, "Body Image and Archaic Thinking" *International J. Psychoanal.* 40 (1959), pp. 223–231.

such activity to break through the uniform roles into which they are locked and to find, despite group life, a way to assert the self?

Many aspects of the relations between self, body image, and pathology have been examined in clinical studies. There have been studies of the body as phallus in both the defense against and the release of strong sexual feelings and excitement.[6] Greenacre associated fetishism with sudden fluctuations in the body image.[7] Schmideberg described the relations between body image and aggression,[8] Bychowski reported on the changes in body image in involutional and schizophrenic states.[9] The literature of hypochondriacal delusions is essentially a literature of body image. Ohyama reports changes in body boundaries under the influence of alcohol.[10] Brenman and Gill described the variations in the modification of the body image during psychotherapy,[11] and Klemperer noted similar phenomena during hypnoanalysis.[12] Peto's adolescent psychotic patients reported experiencing the fusion of their bodies with that of the therapist.[13] They also reported feelings of nothingness, anxiety, or bliss, and fluctuation between haptic kinaesthetic and vestibular sensations associated

[6] Joseph Sandler, "The Body as a Phallus: A Patient's Fear of Erection," *Int. J. Psychoanal.*, 40 (1959), pp. 191–198.

[7] Phyllis Greenacre, "Certain Relationships Between Fetishism and Faulty Development of the Body Image" in R. S. Eissler, et al, eds., *The Psychoanal. Study of the Child* (New York: International Universities Press, 1953), pp. 29–98.

[8] Melitta Schmideberg, "Some Clinical Implications of the Sense of Body Reality," *Int. J. Psychoanal.*, 2 (1953), pp. 207–212.

[9] Gustav Bychowski, "Disorders in the Body Image in the Clinical Picture of Psychoses," *J. Nerv. Ment. Dis.*, 97 (1943), pp. 310–335.

[10] Masahino Ohyama, "Changes of Body Image Boundary Scores under Conditions of Alcoholic Intoxication," *Tohaka Psychologica Folia,* 22 (1964), pp. 100–107.

[11] Margaret Brenman, Merton M. Gill, and Frederick Hacker, "Alterations in the State of the Ego in Hypnosis," *Bull. Menninger Clinic,* 11, (1947), pp. 60–66.

[12] E. Klemperer, "Changes of the Body Image in Hypnoanalysis," *Journal Clinical Experimental Hypn.*, 2 (1954), pp. 157–162.

[13] Andrew Peto, "Body Image and Archaic Thinking," *Int. J. Psychoanal.*, 40 (1959), pp. 223–231.

with changes in the transference relation to the therapist. Peto suggested that these events were elements of an archaic infantile experience which were associated with both the integration of and the modification of the early ego and the formation of the body image. Spitz, in his study of the first year of life, relates the body image to interaction with the mother, to the development of a stimulus barrier, and to learning how to cope with the flooding of stimuli and affect.[14] Failure to achieve a stable body image leads to confusion and failure to differentiate and localize inner and outer dimensions.[15] Eisler held that a defect in integrating a unified body image led the delinquent individual to adopt magical modes in the effort to master his environment and to cope with his unfused self-image.[16]

The use of drugs is one way of manipulating the body image and of shifting the relations between the self and the world. Similar results have been achieved by mountain climbing, skiing, parachute jumping, surfing, and other kinds of kinesthetic and vestibular play. Perception of the genital area as part of the

14 R. A. Spitz, *A Genetic Field Theory of Ego Formation* (New York: Int. Univ. Press, 1959).

15 As Rieff (*The Triumph of the Therapeutic*, New York: Harper & Row, 1966) comments, in examining another aspect of the same problem in his essay on Wilhelm Reich and the new sexuality, "externality is the character without which the portrait of Reich's new man would not be complete." Is it possible that what in an established and ordered world would be classified as "private parts," an element of the interior life, necessarily becomes public and communal in the antinomian world? Does the attrition of ritual compel a return to the orgy, or to group, complex marriage, as that first primitive assertion of communion? The distinction between perversion and "unnatural" acts, on the one hand, and sacred ritual on the other, may be the distinction between private and publicly validated acts, between what exists on the fringes and margin of the group and what is confirmed and legitimated by group membership. Ancient Dionysian festivals and orgies, the orgiastic rites at homosexual public gatherings, or the bacchanalia of the Lenten festivals and Mardi Gras make sense in such a context.

16 Kurt Eisler ed., *Searchlights on Delinquency* (New York: Int. Univ. Press, 1959), pp. 3–25.

body image may in some persons be repressed, become peripheral, or remain ambiguous. Compulsive masturbation and the use of drugs or other devices may serve to cope with this aspect of the body image. "Speed freaks," using amphetamines, often do so for the experience of hypersexuality. Exhibitionism or hyperactive, polymorphous sexual activity are ways to induce and maintain euphoria and to construe the body. Compulsive scratching, burning, and cutting of the skin, reported by obsessive and schizophrenic patients, are other ways to achieve the same end. Similar mediations of the body image may involve such rituals as the hoarding of sputum, skin debris, and mucus, food rituals and avoidances, driven overeating or undereating. I would suspect that a review of the literature on pica, the eating of inappropriate substances, such as clay or chalk, might support hypotheses that this phenomenon is a parameter in the modulation of body image and self. Instead of perversions and abuses of drugs, many individuals substitute yoga exercises and meditation as ways to manipulate body image, shift relations between self, and world to achieve the same or even better "highs."

These various activities achieve not only the discharge of affect but also a specific modification of orientation and attention, especially in the perception of the inner and outer dimensions of the self. If the ego is first a body ego, then such reorientation, contraction and expansion of the sensorium and of the various perceptual subsystems for bodily orientation and balance, for pain, perception of warmth, pressure and touch, for the perception of sound and sight—all originating outside the body—as well as the perception of stimuli arising inside the body become the manipulation, modulation, and modification in the boundaries of ego and of self. The infant, rubbing noses and bumping foreheads with mother, the child on the swing or on the merry-go-round, is beyond play, learning and construing sensation and his body. Drugs and sex games may constitute a regression to this earlier learning—a regression that may be play in the service of the ego. Skiing, the roller-coaster at the amusement park, and the distorting mirrors of the fun house may represent maneuvers to take up and reinstate earlier positions of adjustment and mastery. The distinction between regression experienced as play or as disorganization perhaps marks the difference between the good and bad trips, the latter being experienced as loss of control, as fragmentation of the self and of the cenesthetic matrix on which the self is grounded. Such regressions and manipulations appear to be associated with primitive forms of coping with the environment. Nowadays we can produce the states at will by means of the newer chemical and pharmacological technologies.

In the drug culture there is talk of good and bad vibrations. With its implications of penetration, fusion, influence, and control, this talk is evidence to me of confusion about and threat to body boundaries. Similarly the preoccupation with parapsychology, psychokinesis, and the occult implies problems of body barriers and of penetration, dimensions that have been investigated extensively by Fisher and Cleveland.[17] Similar shifts in the perception of body boundaries may be found in studies of alcoholics who perceive the body as disgusting and decaying. The experience of the permeability of body boundaries has also been studied in patients with arthritis, colitis, and neurodermatitis. The theme of rigidity or lability of body boundaries has been most clearly expressed in the schizophrenics' complaints of influencing machines and of body disintegration. The hyperstimulation and compulsive activity of some sadists, masochists, and homosexuals may also be viewed as efforts to stabilize body boundaries and cope with their permeability.

The new fashions in men's perfumes as well as the importance of hair and of beards[18] may be ways of staking out boundaries

[17] Seymour Fisher and Sidney E. Cleveland, *Body Image and Personality,* 2d rev. ed. (New York: Dover, 1968).

[18] Edgar Stuntz, "The Beard as an Expression of Bodily Feelings in a Schizophrenic," *Psychosomatic Med.,* 21 (1959), pp. 26–33.

for body as well as "soul" and of compensating for the ambiguity of contemporary unisex.

The marijuana user, who puts on earphones and turns the volume high to push the overload of stimuli all the way inside is playing at games of penetration and fusion. In contrast to the passive, receptive, feminine mode, the speed user, sheathed with his tingling skin and orgasmic waves of warmth over his body, senses himself as a penis-bearing animal (as a patient described himself). Users of speed, even in the milder dosages, report continuous secretion of smegma and semen.[19] *Avatar* magazine described the ideal sexual performance as one in which the male was high on speed and the woman was dosed with cocaine. I think a case can also be made that the female speed freak can be experiencing the body as phallus in a masculine mode.

In normal development the body ego as the matrix for the cognitive ego, though it persists as an ongoing surf, remains for the most part unconscious. Scott suggests that the division between body ego and psychic ego is a symptom.[20] When such splits occur, and behavior shifts to the manipulation and modulation of such splits, as in the use of drugs or in sex perversion, we are faced with pathology and efforts to stabilize or reconstitute the self in conditions of stress and crisis. At such times a shift is made from differentiated and individuated cognitive formations, which have been achieved in the process of maturation, to more primitive, more archaic, and more concrete manipulations of the separated

[19] In the underground press ideal sex has been defined as that in which the female is high on cocaine and the male is turned on to methedrine. Conversely, the morphine user is freed from the bondage of sexuality. There are frequent reports of the use of marijuana as an aphrodisiac. As a patient remarked, "Man, with grass you have a hard on all the time." It may be noteworthy that gamblers, not on drugs, report hot waves and flushes diffusing across the belly, the same experience of the body as phallus that morphine users also report.

[20] Scott, "Some Embryological, Neurological, Psychiatric and Psychoanalytical Implications of the Body Schemes"; "The Body Scheme in Psychotherapy."

body ego and psychic ego. In these circumstances hitherto unconscious sensations are experienced consciously. As Scott suggests, the body schema of sensations, perceptions, conceptions, affects, and memories becomes fragmented into shifting figure-ground configurations, which may also move from the interior of the body to the limits of space.

Wapner suggests that drugs undo the polarization and the spatial localization of the body and implies that this involves a regression in the order and structure of behavior.[21] He formulates a dimension of polarization of body-object relations vs. a state of fusion and relates this to such factors as active vs. passive relations between self and object and to Schachtel's differentiation of autocentric vs. allocentric modes of sensory experience and perceptual development.[22] Rierdon and Wapner studied "normal" subjects in their investigations of polarization and fusion. Such studies should also be undertaken with psychopaths, homosexuals, and drug abusers. Wapner states, "similarly for the normal adult under primitivizing drugs like LSD 25, conditions of stress or cases of pathology, where more primitive behavior is evident, the polarization between self and world, which exists for the optimally functioning adult breaks down."[23] Polarity is assumed to be lacking in early childhood and to be a function of maturation. Wapner believes that the condition affecting the degree of polarization between self and object is interdependent with genetic factors such as developmental level, psychopathological status, and other developmental conditions.[24] Separateness, oppositeness, and distance between self and object are characteristics of the more mature individual.

The exhibition and exploitation of the body have been one of

21 S. Wapner and H. Werner, eds., *The Body Percept* (New York: Random House, 1965).
22 Ernest G. Schachtel, *Metamorphosis* (New York: Basic Books, 1954).
23 Wapner and Werner, eds., *The Body Percept.*
24 Ibid.

the salient elements in the counterculture. This has been manifest in a revival of dandyism as well as in the hairy, hang-loose new look. Pornography, topless-bottomless bars, and show business have commercialized the evangelical commitments of nudist camps and naked marathon therapies. Body-painting and talcum-powdering of one another at Saturday night parties have taken the place of strip poker. Blindfolded groping, touching, and shared textural interchanges are conventional procedures in encounter groups, and at meetings of the Sexual Freedom League, orgies are earnestly acknowledged as new rituals of affirmation.

No study of personality is possible independent of an understanding of the society in which the personality exists; the dominant cultural movements, as well as the counterculture reaction to them, are a function of the particular historical and social circumstances in which they develop. Today's youth counterculture, with its emphasis on the manipulation and experimentation of body boundaries and its emphasis on liberation and release rather than on control and adjustment, is a vivid instance of the way in which the body image—as a cognitive construct—and the orientation and values surrounding the body, are to be seen as the expression and extension of the self and as ways of managing the boundaries between the inner and the outer world.

Infancy and early childhood are crucial phases, as the psychoanalysts have demonstrated, for learning and mastering internal stimuli and differentiating these from those arising in the external world. Anomalies in development and psychotic behavior often are expressed as a confusion of the limits between the individual's body and his world and become manifest in the ways in which the disturbed person abuses and perverts his body. It is especially significant that this manipulation of the boundaries of the body—and therefore of the orientation of the individual to the world which can be also achieved through spiritual and religious experiences and through fasting or high fever—occur also with drug use.

In the current diffusion of drugs, such distortions and manipulations of experience, previously known to the extraordinary guru or saint, are now made available as a mass consumer product for everyone, leading to changes in perception of the body, of outside space, of the sense of duration, and of the modification of the thresholds between what is inside and what is outside oneself. The need to manipulate, experiment with, and change the experience of one's own body image, it is suggested, is a product of the breakdown of the stable schemata particular cultures create and is an effort to find and to reestablish adjustment.

V. The Phenomenal Self and the Field

The history of the development of the self, both organismically and across time, has yet to be written. If we were to make such a study, it would be necessary to map a more differentiated self and ego. We still tend to view them in global and undifferentiated terms. It would be necessary to survey not only the inner and outer dimensions of body perception, but also to establish the processes which go into the development of the body-image and its transformation, diffusion, and disintegration. It would also be necessary to specify and delineate the inner and the outer dimensions in the cognitive structures of the ego and the self.

The Making of the Self

We cannot talk about drugs without considering how the self is made and how one relates to one's past and future. It is also necessary to explore how drugs can be used for isolation and retreat or for sacrament and communion, how they can lead either to self-encapsulation or to a new community.

The self is suspended between two poles, and loss of either the inner or the outer anchorage forces the individual into restitutional behavior. We are familiar with the alternatives of the inner-directed man and the outer-directed man as styles of adaptation and accommodation. Either style can be homeless or at home in the universe. What is relevant is that there must be effective commerce between oneself and others. Strategies of hyperactivity or of dropping-out and retreating are devised to reorient and to stabilize the threatened self. When the world of objects loses its stability, people find new ways of thinking as an attempt to restore the stability. The failed rational, cognitive modes based on sight and objectifying are displaced by subjective, intuitive styles and modes of perception that rely on the primitive tactile sense of pressure, temperature, texture, and pain.

Man is neither agent nor pawn. Given a relatively stable surrounding world, he is able to overcome his primary narcissism, symptoms of which are ego inflation and feelings of fusion with the universe. Things identified as spiritual and sacred are usually those in which the self is involved—that is, in which there is an emotional self-investment, collective experience is a meaningful rather than a mechanical activity, and values and meanings are shared within a community.

Psychoanalytic investigators[1] have traced children's interior

[1] Edith Jacobson, *The Self and the Object World* (New York: International University Press, 1964); H. Kohut, "Forms and Transformation of Narcissism," *Journal of the American Psychoanalytic Assoc.* 14 (1966), pp. 243–272; Heinz Lichtenstein, "The Role of Narcissism in the Emergence and Maintenance of a Primary Identity," *International Journal of Psychoanal.*, 45 (1964), pp. 49–56. Leo Spiegel, "The Self, The Sense of Self and Perception," *The Psychoanalytic Study of the Child* (New York: International University Press, 1959), pp. 82–106. D. C. Levin, "The Self: A Contribution to Its Place in Theory and Technique," *International Journal of Psychoanalysis,* Vol.

development from the autistic state, where there is failure to differentiate between subject and object, to that of becoming autonomous and individuated people. They have traced those narcissistic feelings of gratification in which the person invests feeling in objects or representations of the self. A person constructs the image of himself from internal feelings and impulses and from external stimuli. From this interaction emerges reliable boundaries of the self and differentiation of subject and object. Cognitive growth demands precisely this differentiation between inner and outer and between mechanisms of release and control. Ideally a balance between these is achieved. We are all familiar with ways in which one expands or contracts the boundaries of the body and the self. Some people seem to live only behind their eyes and exclude everything below the navel. On the other hand, amputees still experience a phantom limb as present. Some people extend their bodies and their self-concepts into their new red roadsters, their Easter bonnets, the lawn, or the flourish of their signatures. Cognitive growth demands that the infant separate himself from the nurturant, supportive mother, and establish reliable and consistent boundaries which differentiate his wants and wishes from what is outside and independent of himself. He must learn to manage the commerce between himself and the world outside by flexible patterns of control and release so that he can establish and reliably maintain the boundaries of inside and outside. Such a balance ideally is achieved as a function of maturation.

If in childhood this balance is disrupted, sequential development is disorganized and a disordered awareness of the body and its function leads to such clinically identifiable problems as obesity, alcoholism, drug abuse, and the rejection of food. When the

---

50 (1969). Arnold Modell, *Object, Love and Reality: An Introduction to a Psychoanalytic Theory of Object Relations* (New York: International Universities Press, 1968).

individual fails to respond, or responds in contradictory or inappropriate ways to the external world, he loses sense of ownership of his body and control of its functions. In mysticism, drug experiences, and clinical syndromes, we find evidence of similar somatic distortions.

In a stable situation the self achieves constancy as it differentiates itself from all that is not-self. If ambiguity replaces constancy, if others, the not-self, act as a barrier rather than as a reflector and reinforcer, the individual retreats or seeks fusion with the threatening object. In pain he can precipitate consciousness and awareness of self; in rapture, a swoon into the other. Figure and ground dissolve and resolve. His procedures may be ascetic or ecstatic; the issue is the orientation, whether it be outward or inward, field-dependent or independent.

As we view the historical recurrence of antinomian strategies, it appears evident that beside organismic and familial developmental factors, such social parameters as customs, norms, and rituals also operate to reinforce and sustain the experience of the self, its roles, and its construed identity. Perception involves construing objects and differentiating them from the surrounding ground in which they are imbedded. We are all familiar with such illusions, for example, as the drawing which can be seen either as a wine glass or as two profiles depending on which is fixed as figure and which is fixed as ground. In drug experiences and in some behavior disorders, figure-ground relations become unstable and shift and change. The behavior or exercises used may be ascetic or ecstatic; the issue is the matter of orientation whether it is inward or outward, whether it is field dependent and one experiences oneself as subordinate—contained and framed within a single field—or whether it is field independent and one perceives oneself and one's orientation independent of one's surroundings. There is the old yarn about the hunter and his Indian guide who could not find their way back to their base camp: "We are lost, lost," the hunter cried. To which the

Indian replied, ''Me not lost, teepee lost.'' Such orientations of field dependence or field independence seem to be associated with different personality structures, pathological conditions, and with primary cultural orientations.

The stable self incorporates the norms and symbols of the surrounding world and elaborates rituals which serve for man the same function that hereditary instinctive behavior serves for other animals. These rituals provide the regularity for binding and discharging affect; they orient the person and transmit tradition from generation to generation. When rituals and symbols become atrophied and emptied of meaning, when the axis between oneself and others breaks, one either repudiates or loses contact with the other. A frequent consequence is that God is perceived not as the other as that which endures separate from self, but as the self.[2] The elect see themselves as God coming into consciousness. The greater the isolation of this elect, the more they see themselves as chosen. Subject and object fuse into subject, and as we have had occasion to note with Charles Manson and his followers, the immanent God stalks the world.

Manson and his followers, reportedly were fascinated by and

[2] Aberle remarks that drugs are ingested to give a feeling of personal significance to external and internal stimuli. One reaches, not for the vision, but for its meaning and significance in an effort to create and replace the lost continuity and time perspective. In an emptied world one seeks to reestablish the sacred and to reritualize experience. Aberle says, "Peyote is relevant. When a person eats peyote, something external to him proves able to affect his thinking, his feelings, his perception, and his behavior and to do so without his own volition." Drug experience in intensifying the light, making outlines sharper and shadows deeper, makes objects acutely real and "all there." As opposed to the Protestant ethic with its "just don't stand there, do something," the new existentialists say instead, "don't just do something, be there." But what is most noteworthy and significant is that in Indian society, the use of peyote is ritualized and is a group experience. The American, on the other hand, as a trivial recreational user releases the demonic with neither group support nor sanction, and without the awe with which Castaneda's Don Juan respects the demons he evokes. David Aberle, *Peyote* (Chicago: Aldine Books, 1966).

identified with the hero of Heinlein's science fiction novel *Stranger in a Strange Land*[3] and appear to have acted out the ideas presented in that book. Their views like Heinlein's book also parallel typical gnostic values and the libertine orientation of the Brethren of the Free Spirit, one of the leading antinomian heresies of the thirteenth and fourteenth centuries.[4]

Heinlein's book is a dramatization, in a modern urban setting, of gnostic religious views. It combines science fiction with the ethos of an apostolic Christianity and an attack upon established institutions. The protagonist is a human raised by Martians, who is clairvoyant, a master of extrasensory perception and psychokinesis, who enjoys voluntary control of all his bodily functions and is able to free himself of his body at will. The hero expresses an identity with Jesus as the loving son of man and maintains, at the same time, that the elect are beyond sin. Knowing all by illumination and intuition, they are capable of self-actualization in which nothing is forbidden. The moral code merely institutionalizes evil and binds them to a corrupt society which must be surpassed. Members of the group affirm perfect love and perfect sharing and, like earlier antinomian groups, like the Oneida community in nineteenth-century New York, like the group marriage communes developing today, they enter into group marriage in which the sharing of men and women by the entire group is viewed as the marriage of gods. All living creatures are God, and for the gnostic libertine acts, even killing, liberate God from the imprisoning husk of his material body.

In Heinlein's novel the allusion is made to discorporation and Mike, Heinlein's hero, acknowledges that he has liquidated about 450 people and sees this murderous behavior as the act of a referee throwing players out of a game. It was just such a rationalization that Manson, fascinated with the Heinlein story, could

3 Robert A. Heinlein, *Stranger in a Strange Land* (New York: Berkeley Medallion Books, 1969).

4 Paul Zweig, *The Heresy of Self Love, A Study of Subversive Individualism* (New York: Basic Books, 1968).

use as a sanction for his marauding band. Manson, too, could say like Mike who grinned with unashamed cheerfulness, "I am God. Thou art God . . . and any jerk I remove is God too. . . . When a cat stalks a sparrow, both of them are God, carrying out God's thoughts."

This is in the ancient gnostic tradition in which Cain is a hero. The Cainites were an old antinomian sect who honored wicked Old Testament characters like Cain and worshipped the serpent in Eden. Such serpent-worshipping sects, known as Ophites, persist among contemporary witches, too, and in the counterculture in recent years, occult churches, like the Process Church of the Final Judgment and the Solar Lodge of the Ordo Temple Orientis and other satanic groups perform ceremonies that combine sacrifice and orgy. To be freed from the laws of the world is to make possible the liberation of the divine spark in the individual and its return to and fusion with God. It is the assertion of an egotistic self-actualization that repudiates and transcends membership in the world and replaces it with a self-deification in which all acts committed in a state of illumination are only expressions of God manifesting himself.

The loss of membership in a community and a sense of apocalyptic dread or promise support the zealots who do not hesitate now, as in other times, to justify violence in "overthrowing Babylon." The social context of such an orientation evidenced today will perhaps be more readily understood when we compare it with a similar earlier American manifestation of antinomian enthusiasm in the Burned Over District[5] of western New York in the first half of the nineteenth century. After the War of 1812, the invention of the steam engine, the opening of the Erie Canal with its attendant disruption of towns, villages, and their power relations waves of enthusiasm overwhelmed that area. It was in this setting that Swedenborgianism, spiritualism,

[5] Whitney Cross, *The Burned Over District* (Ithaca, N.Y.: Cornell University Press, 1951), p. 244.

mesmerism, phrenology, millennial religions, and Utopian communist colonies committed to group marriage developed and flourished. Many anticipated the second coming of Christ, the end of the world, and the millennium.

Whitney Cross reports an incident similar to the current Manson case:

> Couples had cemented their formerly Platonic affiliation with the new physical sacrament. If rumor can be trusted, Martin Sweet gathered about him near Auburn a household of women, six white and one black; deluded beings, although most of them are well educated and respectably connected, who obey his every whim. The negress is supposed to have been directed to run through the streets with a butcher knife, slaying whatever she met, and three of the white women were reputed to have smashed the communion table during a neighboring service, scattering the cups and drinking the wine.

The concept of the self is considered by some to be marginal in psychology and social psychology. There lingers about it the taint of the "soul" and of the interior homunculus as helmsman. G. H. Mead struggled with the differentiation between self as subject—the "I"—and self as object—the "Me." He spoke of the "I" that reacts to the "me" but tended to overemphasize the social context and to minimize and neglect the role of the subjective aspect of the self. He said, "When the self does appear, it always involves an experience of another; there would be no experience of the self simply by itself."[6]

Sarbin attempted to expand and differentiate Mead's construct.[7] He defined the self as a cognitive structure that functioned as an object for the individual, was learned, and grew

6 G. H. Mead, *Mind, Self and Society* (Chicago: University of Chicago Press, 1934).

7 Theodore R. Sarbin, "A Preface to the Psychological Analysis of the Self," *Psychological Review*, 59 (1952), pp. 11–21.

through specific developmental phases in a process of individuation, regression, or both. But this formulation, too, neglects the functions and role of the internal and subjective self.

Allport has attempted a convergence between the socius, or object self described by Mead, and the proprium, or perceived self (the subjective "I").[8] He differentiated the "I" and the "me" as the polarities of individualism and tribalism.[9] The proprium is the bodily "I." Inner-directed, it does not wait on circumstances; its perception is synthetic and often can be syncretistic rather than discrete. The objects it construes can be highly changeable, are infused with wishes and fears, bound by memory and anticipation, and need not achieve constancy. The proprium functions in a wide arc between autistic and autonomous behavior. At its optimum functioning it successfully synthesizes inner need and outer reality.

Identity and the sense of self are built up as well by stimuli and information from the outer world. This self derived from the outer world was noted by Mead, characterized by Cooley who defined the social self as a "looking-glass self,"[10] and, in its most contemporary formulation, described in the work of the French psychoanalyst and structuralist Lacan who sees the self as the object learned first in the mirror.[11] The self as socius is the person as participant in social behavior who recognizes himself in those values and attitudes shared with others as well as in those which separate him from others. This qualitative experience is grammatical. The "transcendental," as Kant long ago demon-

[8] Gordon Allport, *Becoming* (New Haven, Conn.: Yale University Press, 1955).

[9] Allport maintains, "If the demand for autonomy were not a major force, we could not explain the prominence of negativistic behavior in childhood. . . . All his life long, this being will attempt to reconcile these two modes of becoming, the tribal and the personal."

[10] Charles H. Cooley, *Human Nature and The Social Order* (New York: Scribner's, 1902).

[11] Jacques Lacan, *The Language of the Self* (Baltimore: Johns Hopkins Press, 1968).

strated, cannot be known through sensory experience. Even though one plays the mirror game of infinite regress, from one's body seen, to the seeing eye, from the self and mind to the mind as object of knowledge, perceived by a subject, one comes finally upon the intuited, logical category as a precondition of knowledge. The reciprocal aspects of these two personality structures account for many of the dynamic elements of behavior. Rapaport has commented on some of the symptom systems associated with them.[12]

In addition to the early developmental anchorage in either the proprium or the socius (with typical character and symptom modes), some individuals under stress may require emergency adaptation to one or another anchorage pier of the self. Anxiety can force one to fall back from positions previously taken in either the socius or the proprium, to send emergency help to reinforce a beleaguered position, or to shuttle constantly between them.

In contrast to the alcoholic who uses a drug to direct behavior outside and to facilitate aggression, who extends and augments his socius and anesthetizes and attacks the proprium, the user of marijuana, mescaline, psilocybin, peyote, and LSD falls back upon the proprium in retreat from the socius. He turns back into his own encapsulation to reconfirm his identity in the proprium rather than in the threatening socius and the rejected other. Whenever the world appears too intractable and beyond his capacity to manage or modify, retreat and renunciation become his favored mode. He retreats not only from what is perceived to be externally threatening but disowns as well aggressive and sexual impulses. In his effort to overcome autoerotic and perverse impulses he diffuses them, undoing their differentiated, specific qualities and reflecting them back upon the proprium in a global, undifferentiated, and primitive way.

12 David Rapaport, "The Autonomy of the Ego," *Bulletin of the Menninger Clinic*, 15 (1951), pp. 113–123.

A necrophilic patient demands quiescence from his sex object because movement signifies there are things beyond his control and implies a separation and otherness that are threatening to him. A heroin user on parole informed me that he stays drugged to counteract pedophilic impulses and he fears his preoccupations with the sexual molestation of children. A dried-up drunk or morphine user breaks through with a homicide. These behaviors are instances of the manipulation of inner and outer dimensions in the control and stability of the self.

The turn from socius to proprium involves rejection of the stability and constancy of external objects and seeks gratification in inner rather than outer experiences. Insofar as his experiences become syncretistic, global, and diffused, the threatened person undoes himself. The proprium as self becomes both subject and object, active and passive, agent and agency. Self-encapsulation makes it possible to avoid his own aggression, criminality, and perversion. If one is the agency suffering the intrusion of the agent as foreign substance, one takes distance from one's active role, permits oneself to enjoy the passive surrender, to tolerate the excitement that one disowns as essentially one's own, and to accept the quietude that one invokes as defense. With LSD or marijuana one can listen quietly to the music, displacing the excitation from the self to the projected external milieu, which teems suddenly with invisible "meaning."

One deals with threat by retreat or by identification with the aggressor and assimiliation of the feared object. When the entire self is involved in such an assimilation, its boundaries break down, and one can experience the "union" or "merging" that is reported in mystic experience.[13] The mystic masters his fear of dissolution by merging with the world and denying the boundaries between the me and the not-me. Where the boundaries between socius and proprium are too loose, these maneuvers may

[13] Charlie Chaplin, in "Shoulder Arms," brings in a company of prisoners. Asked how he did so, he shrugs his shoulders and answers, "I surrounded them." But Charlie kept his identity.

not work well, and the aggression turned back from the socius cannot be assimilated. It overwhelms the proprium and a psychotic breakthrough occurs. In an effort to redeem the self and become independent of the external milieu, the drug user elaborates a counterfeit autonomy that makes him instead a victim and slave of the internal milieu. Intending autonomy, he collapses into autism, abdicating the world and renouncing future perspectives for self-absorption and encapsulation.

I have stated the extreme case. Within the normal range are found the normal experiences of the mystic, the aesthetic, and the ecstatic which do not lead to maladaptation and which keep open a functional mobility between proprium and socius. At either extreme there is a constellation of pathological symptoms. The mystic does not represent another order of experience, nor does it differ from the aesthetic. What appears to be involved in the mystic experience is grasping a sense of relationship between disparate elements not customarily seen in the juxtaposition which the mystic or the aesthetic apprehends. If the experience appears indescribable, it is because it involves orders and classes for which the customary rhetoric of daily life has made no provision or because it shifts the conventionally accepted boundaries of the self or time or the typical figure-ground configurations in which we usually maintain the constancy of objects. The mystic and aesthetic experiences permit usually disregarded marginal perceptions to become focal and to displace the selective perception of customarily ordered attention. But, as art demonstrates, these innovations can, in time, become public conventions.

The mystic is in flight from the other in revulsion against his socius. As Zaehner suggests, the mystic is attempting to break through otherness, blurring his identity and individuality, taking distance from the self, and seeking fusion with something extrapersonal.[14] The rhetoric of the mystic probably means, as opera

[14] R. C. Zaehner, *Mysticism, Sacred & Profane* (New York: Oxford University Press, 1963); and *Hindu & Muslim Mysticism* (London: Athlone Press 1960).

tion, giving up one's individual intentionality and will. The mystic maneuver, not as an end but as a means, repudiates affect and appetite. It attempts to overcome a feeling of estrangement and separation anxiety by tossing away the estranged socius. The mystic isolates himself and attempts to unshackle himself from customary memberships and convention and to live in "God's company without care." Like the addict in his encapsulation, euphoria, and ecstasy, who also seeks to divest himself of tension and undo the differentiation and discreteness of experience, the mystic finds in the boundless, companionless, isolated, autistic revery, union and identity with the totality of extension and duration, the universe that the mystics name the "All."

Mysticism for the Brahman consists of isolation, depersonalization, and a concurrent sense of oceanic merging, a totally undifferentiated oneness in which isolation becomes equivalent to identity with the universe. It expresses a yearning, not for the other, but for a changed condition of the self, a release from the socius and its conditional, contingent state. For the true mystic even attachment to God, Zaehner suggests, is an obstacle to liberation. The mystic desires not to love or to unite with God but to emulate him in total detachment from the conditional and in absolute freedom and isolation.

In a secular, naturalistic world that fails to institutionalize the range of roles which other cultures make available, some individuals are forced into deviance and pathology. In our culture drug-taking becomes the secular, private road to the mystic state. We have the junkie; they sanction the holy man. But where the Zen Buddhists acknowledge that sartori, a normal ecstatic experience, is a momentary illumination, the drug user and the LSD cultist seek a steady state of ecstasy.[15]

[15] Edith Jacobson, *The Self and the Object World* (New York: International Universities Press, 1964), says: "Normal experiences of ecstasy do not aim at destruction but are founded on a fantasy of libidinal union between self and object world; they result in a transitory sense

When in times of crisis and transition the reciprocal modes break down and the individual is forced back upon the I, rational cognitive modes based on vision and objectification are displaced by haptic and subjective intuitive styles. Gnostic and antinomian values and techniques return. Hyperactivity and dropping-out are attempts to reorient and stabilize the threatened self. In the struggle between man's "nature" and his need for order, between release and control, issues of man vs. social order, good vs. evil, and God vs. Satan recur.

Allport's formulation implies more than the attempt to account for the role of sensation, perception, memory, and symbolization and the ways in which these interact with the social in constituting the self. Beyond the acknowledgment of becoming as an ongoing process, there linger rumors of ancient polemics between theology and philosophy. Neoplatonists and theologians struggled to separate intelligence from the individual, intending corporeal being. The Neoplatonists saw intelligence invested within the body as "little trapped particles of the divine godhead," that is, parts of an eternal, absolute, transcending intelligence independent of separate people.

Self-actualization, a rallying slogan of the past decade, not only echoes *das Heilige Werden,* the holy becoming of the German *Wandervogel,* but resonates with the old gnostic conceptualizations of the Holy Spirit. In that view the angel needs the response of a soul if his being is to become what it has to be. Self-actualization refers to I, or perfect nature, rather than to me. In comments like "I don't know what's gotten into me" or

---

of self-expansion and the feeling that the self and the world are rich. Such experiences of merging, which may briefly retransform the images of the self and the object world into a fantasy unit vested with libidinal forces, permit an immediate reestablishment of the boundaries between them. By contrast, pathological regressive fusions caused by severe aggression may result in an irreparable breakdown of these boundaries and hence of the self and object representations.

"I am not being faithful to my true self," there is the long shadow of the gnostic Angel Gabriel, the Holy Spirit of the individual reaching for the lost collective other. It is an expression of the individual's alienation.[16]

The dichotomy of the self as subject and object, as agent and agency, is enmeshed in parochial, ideological, and theoretical issues. As long as one is not tied to ideological commitments to a model or to the notion that models are real, rather than merely nominal categories, the principle of complementarity can resolve what appear to be contradictory issues.

If we can transcend the limits of our language which limits us to nouns and permit ourselves instead to construe the self as gerund, as process rather than material category, we may be able to escape from the dualistic formulation of man as agent or agency. Then we could see the issue not as self or ego, but as a selving and coping, which in particular settings establish the locus of control from within or without.

I have elaborated variations upon the theme that the antinomian personality is to be understood as a tuned organism involved in the manipulation of self, sensibility, and body image. Apocalyptic fantasies of the end of the world and agitated, subjective responses to the population explosion and to ecological pollution (independent of their objective substance and validity) may be externalized equivalents of delusions of body disintegration, decay, and diffusion and may be outcomes of the withdrawal of investment from both objects and socius. Self, sensibility, and body image can be manipulated by sexual and athletic activity, by spiritual and yoga exercises, by polymorphous perversions, and, in our technocratic world, by drugs which alter the spatial and temporal locus of the body and the orientation to both the self and the other.

[16] Henry Corbin, *Creative Imagination in the Sufism of Ibn 'Arabi*, Bollingen, Series XCI (Princeton, N.J.: Princeton University Press, 1969).

VI. Ethics, Ethos and Actualization: The Paradigm of the Antinomian Therapies

The intense interest in the marathon and Gestalt therapies is more an expression of a new social movement than of a scientific dialogue. This opinion is reinforced by the assertion, made by a leader of marathon therapy at the 1968 annual convention of the American Psychological Association, that this new movement could remake the world. These therapies differentiate themselves from older therapies by their proud assertion that they are "not detached, cool, and objective"; they encourage "constructive aggression" and "marital fighting" and focus upon and support the active role of the change agent who acknowledges that he finds a stage for his own self-realization. They repudiate conflict models, or social pressure models, and see instead a process that abjures "adjustment" and "insight," or "maturity," for a process of "growth," "risk-taking," and "stepping into the unknown."

What shall we assume about their time perspective? What do they make of past, present, and future? Is the 24-hour marathon therapy session, with its "excitement," "intimacy," and "reciprocity," experienced as immediate involvement and "happenings?"

The last five years have seen a growing enthusiasm and a proliferation of new therapeutic schools and techniques under the banner of encounter therapy, marathon therapy, Gestalt therapy, leaderless, sensitivity training groups, and the behavior therapies. At the same time, criticism of older "established" models and schools has been intensified. We are confronted not only with the enthusiasm of the new practitioners and consumers, but with widespread and mounting concern for the issues of ethical standards in the practice of psychology. The challenge to the validity of the "medical model" (Szasz, Albee and others[1]) and the alternative "sociological," "existential," and humanistic models are fundamental issues that extend beyond the policing functions of a guild or profession.

A rather constricted view, and one that I believe falsifies the underlying problems, orients itself solely to the ethical issue. The following statement appeared in the March 1968 issue of *The American Psychologist*:

> The science and profession of psychology change, and the ethical standards and procedures must reflect such change. Are the ethical standards as currently written sufficient to deal with current practices in consumer and industrial psychology, behavior modification based on principles of learning and reenforcement, and a variety of new group procedures and techniques?[2]

[1] G. W. Albee, The Clinical Psychologist *Newsletter,* Division 12, American Psychological Association, 20 (1968).

[2] Stuart E. Gollan, "Committee on Professional Ethics and Conduct," *American Psychologist,* 23, 2 (1968): 210–211.

In order to consider revisions of the ethical standards, the Committee on Scientific and Professional Ethics and Conduct calls for examples of incidents of current practice so that it can bring its standards up to date. Psychologists have been aware of their need to deal with urgent and changing problems in relation to selective service, the expanding adolescent population, special services associated with drug roles and drug abuse, the sex "revolution," and similar current sources of stress. Many have been dismayed by therapists who offer LSD to adolescent patients or challenge and chide the patient's fear of loss of control. Some have wondered whether the techniques of theater of the absurd and the alienation effects of Brecht are appropriate in the practice in Gestalt therapy, psychodrama, and the encounter therapies.

Partisans of these newer methods have countered such questions by challenging what they construe as the authoritarian role of the "establishment." They invoke rhetorical appeals to academic freedom, to the defense of innovation, progress, and growth, and see themselves as contemporary Galileos confronting the eternal inquisitors of the establishment.

The issue raised by these new modes and the problems that ensue cannot be resolved by procedures that review and modify the ethical code of a profession. Such innovations assert psychological values and roles that are also epidemic in the larger community. Slogans of self-actualization and self-realization have become modish on many campuses and have become a rationale for the hippie scene. The assertion of these values can be seen in the call to the 1968 Annual Workshop of the American Academy of Psychotherapy:

> The theme of the 1968 Annual Workshop is personal (not professional) growth of the psychotherapies—the theme, in brief, of *A New Beginning*. We are proposing in this theme that, in addition to our usual concerns with enlarging technique, and discovering growth-impasses that obstruct our

> work through the encountering that is part of the workshop, that we share with one another our secrets.
>
> The secrets refer to the ways in which we keep ourselves alive, zestful, growing persons in a social system that grinds one down if one lets it; the ways in which we enlarge ourselves as entire persons, rather than letting our social and professional functions devour us. Thus, we hope that people will share and show such matters as ways of becoming more vitally embodied; ways of mediating new ways to be a psychotherapist.
>
> I, for one, believe that the times are calling for a new profession, a westernized version of the eastern guru; the guide and teacher and exemplar who can help oversocialized people get out of their roles and minds and fixated values in order to become "reborn"—again and again and again. I think that we psychotherapists may be the professionals who can most readily grow to that status. At least many of our patients (I now call them "fellow-seekers") are asking us to help them discover new potentialities beyond those activated by usual (or deviant) socialization. I believe we can best train ourselves experimentally, through encounters with gurus of our own choosing, through various "ways of growth," and through sharing our findings and experiences.[3]

Can we cope with the issues raised by this appeal within the framework of ethical problems and the modification of an ethical code? Shall committees review ethical codes with each new-look therapeutic procedure? An ethical code that is so tendentious that it reflects only short-term goals and standards quickly be-

[3] Sidney Jourard, Department of Psychology, University of Florida.

comes obsolete. It is open to question whether we are confronted with an obsolete and inadequate code or whether the issue, as an "ethical" problem, is a pseudo-issue that displaces the basic problem and deflects us from the significant area of concern. An ethical code for effective governance cannot be a particularized manual. Rather, it should assert broad and general values central to the profession and the community of which the profession is a part. It should be an open-ended system defined ideally not by specific rules, but by the accumulation of cases and traditions in a "common law."

Whether techniques are modified or innovations are assimilated, it should be possible to affirm the central and basic values of a profession independent of "schools." Unless these basic values are themselves challenged such a consensus is possible. A code based upon commonly held values can define a body of principles rather than regulations. Certainly there should appear to be common assent to such principles as that the welfare of the client is the primary concern of the professional psychologist. The psychologist is always concerned with safeguarding his client's welfare and will never act in an exploitative or self-aggrandizing way in relations with his client. Principles further can establish boundaries of competence and integrity that delineate the components of adequate training with the knowledge available in the field. They also can acknowledge that the profession as the guardian and transmitter of knowledge and as the source of sanction that gives the individual his authority, his status, and his license must be protected. This is not to assert merely guild behavior and guild standards. To protect the identity of a profession is to protect and keep uncontaminated the profession's source of knowledge.

Such a view is defensible when shared and common values do exist. If psychologists share a common vocabulary and model and if their procedures and operations are accepted as derived from such a model, they would not be forced into polemical issues formulated as the defense of academic freedom or of innovation and creativity against the vitiating bonds of the bureaucratic "establishment." Certainly such abuses are potential. We are aware, for example, despite Freud's views about nonmedical psychoanalysts, of the guild practices of the American Psychoanalytic Association.[4] The attacks against the innovative procedures of Sister Kenny in the treatment of poliomyelitis are cited as an example of the dangers of such reactionary political power that tries to pass as the defense of science. And we are often reminded by the new enthusiasts of Freud's struggle against the established university and clinical authorities. But, if this last instance is to be used to make a case, it should be clear that the issue was not an ethical problem but the introduction of a new paradigm that altered the fundamental perspectives of the scientific community.

If we examine Jourard's appeal for a new profession and his call to become "reborn," we are confronted not with the problem of ethics, but with a rejection of the central ethos that makes the fabric of meaning for a culture. The new therapies can be understood as symptoms, not as treatment procedures. They express an antinomian crisis in psychotherapy which is similar to that expressed in the drug and sex scenes and in existential theologies and resurgent mysticism. In some professional circles Tarot cards and astrology are accepted as offering a valid conceptual framework for the study of man.

We are not concerned with the problem of quacks who offer shortcuts and panaceas. Such problems are perennial, and attempts to curb quacks' activities and to protect the public are always ineffective because those who seek magic will continue to find ways to bestow their patronage. Nor are we faced only with the same old resistances and hostility to the constructs of psycho-

[4] Ernst Federn, "How Freudian are the Freudians?" *Journal of the History of Behavioral Sciences* (July 1967), pp. 269–281.

analysis. We always have these with us, though they may now use the new modes to reinstate the discarded techniques of suggestion, abreaction, and catharsis. (Some of the new psychotherapies use techniques of rapid intervention, but these procedures often depend upon inferences derived from psychoanalysis.)

We are instead considering those new therapies which are a flight from psychoanalysis. These therapies are a response to the disappointment and overenthusiastic acceptance of psychoanalysis in the 1930s and 1940s, when psychoanalysis was becoming Americanized. The new therapies seek solutions in either technocratic scientism or in recoil from rational secular values, both of which are part of the climate of this time.

The alienation is apparent when the underlying issues of ethics and the new therapies question the validity of the parameters within which psychotherapy has customarily operated. Wordsworth defined poetry as ''emotion remembered in tranquility.'' This statement, I believe, can stand as well as a definition for psychotherapy. In a culture in equilibrium mutuality of contact is assumed. It does not have to be improvised or extracted by exercises of touching, rehearsals of role-playing, or the pseudo-communion of orgies. In a stable culture the self is defined as much by its limits and renunciations as by its releases and discharges. It does not seek epiphanies and actualization. When the culture is not questioned, both patient and therapist accept as given the structure of the world and the legitimacy of their assigned status and role position. They see their task as finding a way back into the social fabric that is the ''nature'' of the world and of ''natural'' behavior.

The problem at the heart of the nihilistic ethos, the other face of enthusiasm and mysticism—and this is the crucial issue, not the technology of psychotherapy—is the repudiation of ideas, abstractions, and theories that give meaning to a universe. The myths and rituals by which man construes his person and his place have lost their power. Nietzsche described the situation as that which occurs "when man begins to doubt cognitive modes of experience and the law of causation seems to suspend itself."[5] The individual's body image is threatened with dissolution, his spatial sense and identity becomes ambiguous and unstable, and his figure-ground relation to his surroundings becomes confused and uncertain. It is a process of depersonalization and unselving. The hippies themselves speak of "ego death."

It is in this context that we must consider the return to the abreaction model and the rejection of rational insight-at-a-distance perspectives. It is not only disappointment with the results of psychotherapy[6] that is the issue, but also the loss of morale and the transvaluation of ethos. A professional and scientific transaction would be an expression of analytic rigor rather than of ideology and morale. It would systematically scrutinize "anomalies" and try to account for them on theoretical grounds. Modifications in procedure would be a function of corrections in theory as these anomalous incidents were incorporated within an adequate theory.

If we see the issue as one of an ethical code, which sections must we change? What do we wish to modify in the definition of acceptable and good practice? What are the changing boundaries of integrity and competence?

Kuhn's study *The Structure of Scientific Revolutions* argues that "normal science" presupposes a conceptual and instrumental paradigm accepted by an entire scientific community.[7]

Kuhn remarks that "normal science proceeds without rules only so long as the relevant scientific community accepts without

[5] Friedrich Nietzsche, *The Birth of Tragedy* (New York: Doubleday, 1956).

[6] To properly assess the "failures" we would have to concede that training has been inconsistent and often inadequate, that standards have not been clearly defined or adhered to, and it could be argued that there is little room for disappointment since the "established" systems have not really been tried because of inadequate training.

[7] Thomas S. Kuhn, *The Structure of Scientific Revolutions* (Chicago: University of Chicago Press, 1962).

question the particular problem-solution already achieved." It is clear that rules and standards of practice are a function of the underlying model invoked and that rules become an issue whenever models are challenged. It is such a situation that we now face. The new modes in psychotherapy express, beyond the customary resistance, processes which reflect both a direct expression of the contemporary ideological crisis and some positive factors that are a measure of the changing perspectives of the scientific community. If we can differentiate these factors, we can more effectively clarify the issues of ethics, ethos, and methodology.

He examines the crises which cannot be resolved within these models and the ways in which these lead to new models and refinements of theory. His historic examination and the regularities he posits in the development of scientific changes are relevant to our present concerns and can illuminate our problems.

According to Kuhn, problems, standards, and legitimate methods are perceived univocally when one model is dominant. Schools become differentiated when standards, methods, and choice of problems are under attack and the validity of the stabilized model is challenged and debated. The more precise and meticulous the model, the more sensitive an indicator it provides of those anomalous results which theory may not have predicted or cannot account for. It is in an attempt to account for these anomalies that theoretical and procedural modifications that lead to the change of the paradigm are undertaken.

In examining the psychological innovations now being promulgated, we must question the systematic context from which they derive and the anomalies in experimental and clinical data of which they are aware and which they believe the established models cannot explain. What are the refinements in theory and in prediction and explanation that these innovative procedures claim to achieve?

Kuhn notes that one measure of a scientific crisis and one of its typical effects is the tendency to return to elements antecedent to the established model. The reversion to systems of abreaction, suggestion, and catharsis, questioned since the 1920s, is an expression of the crises facing the psychotherapeutic model. Usually a novel theory emerges after pronounced and persistent failure of the paradigm in the normal problem-solving activity in which the discipline is engaged. But in psychology, given the variability of our training and the competition between schools, can we assert that failure is a function of the model? Or is it the range of training standards in the various "schools?" Given data can be subsumed under alternate theoretical constructs, and so long as the tools work adequately, one is not compelled to seek alternatives. The demand for retooling, the blurring of the paradigm, and the loosening of the rules for normal research are other indicators of the developing crisis. The crisis will be resolved with the emergence of a new paradigm.

Kuhn demonstrates that the crisis period in these scientific revolutions is marked by individual, eccentric, estranged behavior. Practitioners commit themselves to new perspectives and new institutional frameworks. Polarization occurs, communication breaks down, and there is no longer a shared vocabulary or framework to adjust differences. Does the question of ethics arise when the real issue is the choice of competing, or incompatible, models which we have failed to make explicit? The choice cannot be determined by evaluating procedures of the "normal" model since it is the model which is the issue. As a consequence, we become involved in sterile, futile polemics and debate. Each group uses its model to argue in its model's defense, invokes the rhetoric of polemic and persuasion rather than evidence, and asserts aesthetic orientations rather than data. Instead of talking of logic and evidence, they offer testimonials and manifestos.

Models have normative as well as cognitive functions. The facts, operations, and measurements that scientists manipulate are not raw data, "given" in experience. They are an abstraction, which is preselected as a function of a specific model, and a product of specific styles of perception. As Kuhn observed, "Far more clearly than the immediate experience from which they in part derive, operations and measurements are paradigm-determined." It follows then that scientists with different paradigms engage in different manipulations. Their activity and perception is rooted in constructs. Different models involve differently ordered universes. "Proponents of competing paradigms practice their trades in different worlds; they see different things when they look from the same point in the same direction."

Kuhn concludes that neither proof nor error is at issue. The transfer of allegiance from one to another model is essentially a conversion experience. Resistance to such conversion is not necessarily a violation of scientific standards; it is an expression of the feeling that the older model will solve the problems and puzzles and that by precise work the difficulties can be isolated and overcome. This "orthodoxy" can only be countered if it can be demonstrated that the new model solves anomalies, quantifies more precisely, and is more elegant.

Antinomian Therapies.

Have the new therapies, as alternatives to the traditional methods, offered such data, or have we heard instead testimonials that tell more of evangelical zeal than they do of scientific conduct? The new therapies, with styles and values consonant with the current hippie ethos, are themselves more symptoms than cure.

Modish ideologies of self-actualization and self-realization encourage experimentation with drugs, sexual hyperactivity, and spiritual exercises in the name of new life styles to counter the loss of boundaries, the identity confusion and diffusion that are parts of the process of unselving and renewal with which the drug counter culture is involved.

In humanist and existentialist therapies, "marathon" and "encounter" groups, and sensitivity training self-help groups, pathology and acting-out find sanction. We cannot speak of specific procedures and techniques of intervention and their underlying strategies until we differentiate psychotherapy as ideological commitment from psychotherapy as theoretically grounded scientific procedure.

The choice of therapist or therapeutic school is often an irrational procedure. It may be the expression of the symptom and the choice of defense. Some individuals do seek therapists and modes within the Establishment and indicate by their choice their wish to reject certain roles. Others turn to the "new-look" therapies not so much to initiate a "cure" as to legitimate their acting-out and to find a larger stage upon which to amplify their symptoms. These therapies offer the same alienation disguised as affect and the same uprooting rationalized as acts of release and pseudo-control. Unless a case can be made for homeopathic strategies in psychotherapy, these procedures are more malady than remedy.

One of the fundamental axioms of "established" psychotherapy is that therapy takes place within a framework of deprivation and that the patient's wishes are not to be indulged or gratified. It is characteristic of the antinomian therapies that they are driven to overcome insensibility and unselving by indiscriminate consumption of sensations.

The devouring of sensation is a characteristic hippie motivation. It is reflected in the phrase to be "turned on," whether to another person, to faceless sex, to drugs, to rock and roll, or to God. Because one is essentially uninvolved, one reaches, by means of drugs, light shows, or rock and roll, for immediacy and a sense of presence. If one can achieve a sense of presence, one can then establish both the field and the boundaries of the self.

One of the flower children in the Haight-Ashbury, an eager spectator to the drama of fire engines, ladders, and a burning building, exclaimed, "Wow, I smelled *real* smoke!" Similarly, I heard a hippie eagerly exclaim, "I tasted tear gas!" Such primitive responses indicate either stimulus hunger or an effort to overcome the refractory phase produced by satiation. They represent one form of the "peak experiences," of the "B type of cognition," to which Maslow refers.[8] Maslow and these hippies all refer to the total attention, fascination, and absorption in which "the figure becomes all figure and the ground, in effect, disappears" and in which "the percept had become for the moment the whole of Being." Both express syncretic thinking, fusion, and isolation rather than individuation, differentiation, and objectification. Maslow defines a "peak experience" as a situation in which the subject "perceives the world as if it were independent of him and of all human beings." This is not so much a definition of a peak experience as of a "happening" in an empty field.

Individuation is one of the basic goals of therapy. But individuation (and differentiation of self and object) requires postponement, delay, inhibition, and time binding—all of which are necessary to achieve a social self, control over impulses, and capacity to cope with objects.

Today, as in former times of turbulence, values are shifting and unstable, and cognitive modes of experience and laws of causality appear to be suspended. The givenness of the appropriate ratio of impulse gratification and control is challenged. A sound theory of therapy makes a place for release and control. It seeks the widest range of both individuation *and* socialization.

Therapy that is oriented toward the release of impulses focuses on the private self. Therapy oriented toward control focuses on the social self and its relation to the community of others. All therapies place themselves on the continuum between these two

[8] Abraham A. Maslow, *Towards a Psychology of Being* (Princeton, N.J.: Van Nostrand, 1962), pp. 70–72.

poles. In my opinion, the ideal therapeutic system is one which permits the widest range.

It is no longer fashionable in the circle of naked marathon therapy to maintain that it appears to be a useful therapeutic goal to support the growth of the ego as administrator and negotiator between impulse and the other, rather than to encourage total surrender to impulse or total submission to the other. Therapy implies a system of mediation rather than merely games of release. But to what ends and what goals? Accepting status and role position as "natural" requires the internalization of a culture. When commitment to a plausible and viable public can no longer be acknowledged, the orgy becomes the basis for communion and the prototype of the community. Private "rights" supersede civic "rituals."

The antinomian character, a product of both alienation and loss, is an adaptive groping towards new forms of value and integration. It is expressed in the ideologies of confrontation and encounter therapy, in many of the alleged sensitivity-training sessions in which blindfolded subjects grope for texture and touch in a charade that mirrors their actual disorientation and loss of "contact," and in marathon therapies that encourage physical assault and examination of the secretions of nose and ear.

Proponents of self-actualization maintain that their ethos is to replace the ethos of the "well-adjusted man"; the self-actualizer would become the ideal for our age as the saint, the hero, the gentleman, the knight and the mystic were for other ages. But it should be noted that these earlier images are defined in terms of roles, whereas the self-actualizer has no functional role and no referent other than the encapsulated self. It is this lack of role definition that characterizes the antinomian character and the underlying alienation. The uprooted self is either spectator or possessed actor, but the interrelated functions of self as agent and self as agency remain unbridged.

The demand that one remain true to one's reified, inner nature (that pure spirit imprisoned in the flesh) is an assertion that can grow only out of a polarization and rupture of the constructs of self and other. This demand tells more about the politics of confrontation and encounter than about a psychology of the self and the ways it develops in a social field.

If words like "self" and "transcendence" are to be assimilated into a scientific vocabulary and dialogue, rather than echoing an ancient gnostic dualism, they must have a social reference. And if, as an achievement of self-actualization or self-realization, one is to transcend the person, can transcendence mean anything other than self-limitation, the accommodation to the other, and the awareness and consciousness that are a function of this limitation? As Schachtel remarks, "the doubt and search for identity always go together with alienation from others and from the world around us," and "the preoccupation with reified identity directs attention away from what [one] *does* to what [one] supposedly *is* and releases one from responsibility and obligation."[9]

It is a basic goal of all schools of psychotherapy to help the individual achieve perspective, to see himself as others see him, to differentiate the components of the self as the spectator and actor, and to distinguish the self as agent from the self as agency. Perhaps the key difference is that where older therapies speak of differentiation, the self-actualizing therapies imply dissociation and see dissociation as a positive value. Self-actualization, or the psychology of being, appears to be enmeshed in a dualistic ethos. On the one hand, self-actualization seeks to overcome primitive, behavioristic, stimulus-response models and to replace them with an organismic orientation and a systems approach to the study of personality. If self-actualization sustained such a position, it might help create that psychology of affect of which we still understand so little. Instead, it becomes entwined, and is even

[9] Ernest Schachtel, "On Alienated Concepts of Identity." *The American Journal of Psychoanalysis,* 121, 2 (November 1961): 120–131.

further distorted by its enthusiastic disciples, in a secular evangelism that in the encounter therapies is committed solely to drive-release and expressions of other-directed conformism. A vocabulary influenced by and borrowed from Maslow is used to justify modes of diffusion and release and strategies of kicks and being turned-on. If the intention was to reassert the values of impulse acceptance and to clarify the fears people have in encountering and acknowledging their drives, these values would be within the mainstream of psychotherapy and its psychology. But instead, the gnostic bias leads alternately to hyperactivism, detachment, and to quietism. In maintaining that they are living rather than preparing to live, the self-actualizers become constricted to a psychology of "spontaneous" happenings. Their hedonism is associated with the sense that they cannot really influence their lives. Fatalism dons hedonistic clothes, and they bow to "destiny" and toy with an astrology that is half shamefaced conviction and half put-on. As they say, "Everyone has his Karma."

The less bizarre of the new therapies do call to our attention the fact that therapy is not an informational and explanatory process alone, but an emotional experience and resolution. But an emotional experience implies no *folie à deux* and no reciprocal, symmetrical interchange. Verbal, analytic, conceptual devices may not be the only means for inducing conduct reorganization and behavior change. But the appeal to raw experience prior to concepts and abstractions merely involves other implicit concepts and abstractions which, since they remain unexamined, may be even more vitiating. Among these implicit concepts are the reified self, its biologic and nonsocial nature,[10] an à priori commitment to the Dionysian as opposed to Apollo-

[10] Even the self-taught psychotherapists of Synanon know better when they insist that communication and a sense of community are central to the therapeutic process. "Community means abandoning self as separate. No more I and you because there is no I without you." *The Synanon Scene*, 8 (1968).

nian values, and a psychology of release, abreaction, and catharsis that is a reversion to the cruder techniques of the early years of the century. Old resistances return in the name of innovation.

An "old saw" has it that one pays the doctor because he knows what not to do. As I listen to the enthusiasm of my students speaking of self-actualization and self-realization, it seems important to call attention to these ideological movements as dead ends rather than as progressive developments in psychotherapy or psychology. Even before naked marathon therapy, it was possible to report on the Emperor's new clothes.

The hippie scene requires no new techniques or special modifications. As I have suggested, the choice of therapist or school is itself often symptomatic. If the therapist is sensitive and tactful, he always refrains from imposing his own values and biases. But what is crucial is the achievement of a mutuality that is usually assumed in a culture but which can no longer be taken for granted. And most important, it cannot be wooed by substitutes of physical touch and gratification. Mutuality can be achieved in the quiet offer of acceptance and of recognition of the patient's otherness just as it can be lost and disrupted if the therapist is critical and frightened and has to impose "establishment" values on the patient. It can also be lost when the boundaries between patient and therapist break down. We should adopt the rule of the life guard at the public beach, "Reach, throw, row—then go." One need not agree with the patient so long as one hears what he says and recognizes him. But even more important, one must acknowledge the need for a unitary system of belief which is the ground of a culture, and for a common vocabulary for personal and corporate existence which defines *identity* and *public* and *membership*. Both patient and therapist must honestly commit themselves to this task.

Postscript: A Picture for the Exposition

Maneuvers of conversion and transcendence, which seek to abandon the chrysallis of the old self transform and resynthesize a deranged self and find for it new anchorage points, may take the form of a cargo cult awaiting glad tidings or appear as a reverse cargo cult—a dumping syndrome—which repudiates privilege, position, and wealth and goes forth to the people.

We have cited some of the historical instances in which the antinomian personality has construed and has improvised the frame of reference which it requires as sanction and as support. Communes, whether they are committed to handicrafts and retreat to the countryside or whether they are conspiratorial Weathermen, are flourishing. They seek a new ethos of socialization as well as a flight from boredom, banality, and privilege. Their members trade their internalized conscience for an externalized, sanctioning agent that dilutes or dissolves the individual superego and allows and encourages desublimated acts that the unsupported individual could not initiate or sustain.

There are many points of entry into communes and extended "families." Some come from the shared work and political experiences of the civil rights struggle in the south, or from the shifting roles in the drug culture. Many of the hundreds of students who joined the Venceremos Brigade to harvest crops and cut sugar cane in Cuba, returned with a vision and the determination to build a new man, free of egoism and chauvinism. These students see politics, not as an avocation distinct from their personal life, but as a central organizing principle in which public and private fuse and in which the private experience is held to be a failure of nerve and a lapse from faith. For these people there can be no separation of work from belief; faith and work become one. They reject careers and credentials, find living with one person lonely and alienating, and improvise—often with group marriage, new supportive families, and communities.[1] Though they are reacting to fundamental problems of

[1] Carol Brightman's life-style changed after her experience in the Venceremos Brigade. Previously, she had spent her time studying for her master's degree in American studies at the University of Chicago, teaching at various eastern colleges, editing an antiwar magazine and doing free-lance writing. All successfully. Politics had been distinct from her means of survival and personal life.

Since her return from Cuba, that separation no longer exists. She said she found living with just one person (her husband) functioning as a professional writer—her husband also wrote and taught—was alienating and lonely.

"I eventually ran out of motivation to energize myself. I feel it is necessary to build a new kind of family, a new kind of supportive community with radical institutions that answer people's needs."

Carol now lives in a communal house in Berkeley with five other people. Everyone eats together, shares marketing and housework, pays rent according to his or her ability.

No longer does she see herself as an affluent, middle-class white woman,

the contemporary world, they are not providing effective and adequate solutions. Often, as a result of their rejection of rationality, they turn to an absorption with the occult and to fascist solutions.

One such group is "the Family" organized by Mel Lyman, a former computer technician and prominent jazz banjoist. He evidently is a leader of great charismatic potency who appears to be moving from an earlier quietistic orientation toward a new militancy in which he promises to change the world.

Lyman first organized a commune at Fort Hill Park in Roxbury, Massachussetts in 1966. That group, recruited from the Boston underground counterculture, expanded in a short time to occupy most of the dwellings surrounding Fort Hill Park. Spiritual insights and religious experiences led them to transcend drug roles and to find a new ground for meaning and being. Lyman said he was the avatar of the Living God and was so accepted by his followers. He said he was on a mission from another planet. In the confusion and the frustrating politics of the mid-1960s, a despairing time that saw the assassination of John F. Kennedy and Martin Luther King and an end to the dreams associated with them, Lyman's followers eagerly accepted him as god and as head of their family.

Many of them had used the stimulant benzedrine by day and the tranquilizer Miltown by night. Later they used more complicated drugs, and under the influence of LSD, they found an intense disruption and reorganization of their orientation, which they experienced as a conversion. In the underground newspaper *Avatar*, which his group published from Boston, Lyman's views were broadcast:

---

she said. By removing herself from Middle America, she has been forced to deal with a new reality: Lack of money and the loss of privileges that she had as a member of the white middle-class Establishment.
San Francisco Chronicle, October 31, 1971, p. 13.

> The time for drugs is now past. Those for whom these mind openers were sent are already gone to work. They are building communities, establishing communications, leading their people and their simple values back into the open after an embryonic time. . . . They create order amid confusion, simplicity amid complication, truth and clear sight where lies and blindness rule.
>
> The time for drugs is now past. It should be let go. New work is here, making concrete the unity we have seen, with or without drugs.[2]

But his sense of unity and religious experience were at times overwhelmed by a euphoric ego inflation. At one time he limited his divinity: "I am God only in the sense that I am one with the spirit of God. The Father is in Me and I know Him well. He is my leader as I am yours. . . ."[3] In another issue, a photograph showed the old revolutionary tower that stands on the highest point of land in Boston, like a giant phallus thrust up against the heavens, and in his enthusiasm Lyman declaims:

> *"I am going to fuck the world*
> *I am going to fill it with hot sperm*
> *Mmm, Mmm I can't wait*
> *I am a giant erection*
> *I am all "cock."*
> *. . . and the world*
> *is all "cunt."*

As an avatar he has claimed to be Buddha and Jesus and has spoken in Sufi terms about man. His comments move from an existential pathos, nostalgia, and hurt and seem to shift into the denunciations of superman who threatens to destroy and to re-

[2] *Avatar*, p. 9.
[3] *Avatar*, December 22, 1967.

new the world. The quietistic pilgrim and lover has turned into the anabaptist avenger. Instead of the God who is immanent in every man, Lyman eventually said, "I am going to operate as the heart and center, putting into effect a world government."[4]

The loving Jesus and Buddha says in his "Declaration of Creation":

> *I am going to burn down the world.*
> *I am going to tear down everything that cannot stand alone.*
> *I am going to turn ideals to shit*
> *I am going to shove hope up your ass*
>
> *I am going to reduce everything that stands to rubble*
> *And then I am going to burn the rubble*
> *And then I am going to scatter the ashes*
> *And then maybe someone will be able to see SOMETHING*
> *as it really is.*

He protests that he is not better than anybody else. It is that he represents the best in everybody and that he is only "telling it like it is." "People have to get together and love one another, I mean really FEEL each other," and in a martyr's messianic stance, he appeals, "CURSE me. HATE me! Do something real."

The capitalized words indicate his feelings. His nihilistic and loving frenzy doesn't seem to put off his followers. What in other circumstances might be ascribed as paranoid posturing, becomes within the sensibility and ethos of the hippie scene a program worthy of credence. He can assume a role legitimated by his supporters in which he can announce:

> I DO know everything, everything that MATTERS. I know the human heart . . . what it needs and how it is achieved. I know God's plan and I will reveal it to mankind, step-by-step as God reveals it to me . . . I fully comprehend

[4] *Avatar,* undated and unnumbered issue, approximately March 16, 1968.

> the history of mankind and, . . . where we are going. Within the scope of my consciousness is all that man has ever known and more. I know the next step in evolution and how to bring it about. I alone know these things and only through me will they be known. I am the bridge between God and Man, I am Christ.[5]

His righteousness and zeal do not alienate his followers. In five years his family has grown to a following that numbers two hundred, and new communes have been founded in New York City and in Los Angeles. These family members are by no means cranks; among them are productive artists, musicians, and actors. Lyman usually lives in isolation, and no one meets him who is not already a committed worshipper and follower. He seems clearly to be moving toward a new kind of antinomian politics.

In an issue of *Avatar* he wrote an appreciation of Tim Leary:

> I am thinking about how much credit Tim deserves for turning on a whole generation of misfits. I'm thinking about all the boobies who go around poormouthing the man who put acid in their mouths and flowers in their hair, and I don't even like the bastard myself, but I sure give him a lot of credit, he worked his ass off for a long time to get the LSD thing off the ground. . . . It's not true that I don't like him, actually I love him, he's got a lot of guts, I just wish he was a greater man than he is so that he would accept the responsibility of the leader. . . .[6]

By July 1967, Lyman denounced the hippie lack of self-discipline: "There is more truth in President Lyndon Johnson than in all the Learys and Ginsbergs. . . . If there is more truth in a southerner, HATING a negro than in a hippie loving him, then I am for the southerner. . . . WAKE UP. . . ."

[5] *Avatar,* March 1968.

[6] Leary, himself, had no doubts about his leadership. He said at the time of his escape to Algiers, "Tell them I'm a leader—like Sartre."

This is the man who presents himself as Christ in person[7] and says he will turn the world upside down. He seeks to integrate all the little communes spread over the country into one greater community and appeals to them to be New Christians and transform the world by fighting for love.

This coercive lover seems to have no confusion about discipline and authority. The Lyman family has a karma squad that enforces discipline, and recently, when a commune member made off with an automobile belonging to the group, the karma squad pursued, apprehended him and returned him to custody at Fort Hill. In a conflict with the staff of Pacifica Foundation's FM radio station KPFK in Los Angeles, members of this commune used force in a manner reminiscent of Nazi storm trooper style. Force also was used on an earlier occasion, when an issue of *Avatar* was seized by Lyman's disciples at the time that an editorial board, independent of Lyman, split off and undertook to continue publication of the paper.

The fury of Lyman's love grows greater. He now hates hippies, hates the old generation, hates Women's Lib, and hates "the empty faggots," and he asserts that "I guess the only people I love any more are cops, they warm my heart." Ruefully he writes: ". . . Once there was great hope in our youth, we even mildly anticipated a revolution, the hippies were going to SAVE THE WORLD. But they all died . . . the blacks went middle-class, the hippies went out into the woods and turned into trees. The world is dying and I refuse to die with it."[8]

He has another plan: "I'm gonna get up an army of all the people in this world who still have balls enough to fight this creeping decay, and we're gonna go around raiding all you creeps, and there ain't nothing you can do about it, just sit on your beards and wait for us to come."

7 *Avatar*, No. 4 (July 21, 1967).
8 Richard Herbruck (a name Lyman used for his manifestoes), *LA Free Press,* June 11, 1971, p. 2.

The rhetoric of exasperation and violence is easily triggered, and he sounds not too unlike the radical right when he says, "You're stinking up the whole world with your filthy hair, and dirty clothes and empty slogans and phony smiles. It's over man, you didn't make it. Why don't you kill yourself?"

The radical right, or Manson? If one takes a long enough journey, one comes round the farther pole.

Sometimes his messianic fervor and the ego inflation are displaced by desolation and loss and then he says: "I'm a living, feeling, dedicated human being all alone on a big dead planet." Or wrath takes the place of the lost love:

> I don't want to save the world anymore, there ain't nothing worth saving. I just want to do God's WILL. God is angry at you, I know, he tells me so. You killed Him. You stuck a joint in his mouth and put him out to pasture, you palmed him off on your friends as "peace and love." You made a mockery of His Great Strength. You crucified him in HIS NAME. But he'll get you, he ain't that easy to lay aside, he's inside you now and mad as hell. You forgot about HIS WRATH. He'll make a Big Earthquake and swallow you all up—ideas and all. And he's inside ME. He makes my heart pound He's so big inside me. He's coming back, and not like you thought he would, he's coming back MAD. HE IS THE GREAT DESTROYER."[9]

In the spiritualist and lover lurks the destroying angel, and like the Weatherman and the Manson family, the Lyman family exposes its latent structure of violence and rage. The innocents of the love generation gird their loins and turn newly discovered plowshares into swords. As in earlier romantic and antinomian movements which come around full circle to value medievalism and tradition and find identity interchangeable with Nature or

[9] David Felton, "The Lyman Family's Holy Siege of America," *Rolling Stone*, No. 99 (January 6, 1972).

God or the all-powerful state, this newest manifestation reveals how quickly the corporate identity of a Black Mass can be converted into membership in the elite Black Shirts, how the new acid wafer of communion finds a less symbolic and more explicit communion in a blood brotherhood. The Weathermen, in their first reaction to the news of the Manson murder, hailed Charles Manson as a persecuted leader of the counterculture. The Jesus freaks attack those they deem to be in league with the devil.

The foregoing papers were written at varying times during the past decade and reflect my own changing adjustments and evaluations of the drug culture. During the present decade the culture continues to change from month to month, and leaders of the drug movement have, in some instances, come full circle from the position at which they first began. In the beginning, the politics was that of abdication and retreat, of despair about Vietnam, of flight from decaying cities, of impotence before an unresponsive authority, of flower children who disdainfully said, "politics is not my bag." Timothy Leary, as a California prisoner identified with the Weathermen, saw himself as a new political leader in Algiers, and today has become an exile in Switzerland. Ken Kesey, the merry prankster, who seemed in the early years of drug culture to be most concerned with mocking the squares and the Establishment and who formed an alliance with the Hell's Angels, seemed for a time most clearly to point toward that adventurism which had led earlier romantics toward authoritarian and fascist roles. Now he has reemerged from the silence and retreat of Oregon to say, "You might think that politics is against the nature of the counterculture, but nothing is more important to me in my soul's progress through the universe, and I can't have a beautiful trip while others are starving."[10]

He staged fifteen political happenings in two weeks and is

[10] *Daily Californian,* Vol. 11, No. 42 (March 7, 1972) p. 1.

forming a political party which will include John and Yoko Lennon and Allen Ginsberg as allies. As a result of these Kesey happenings, there have been organized an Armadillo party in Texas, a Crazy party in Delaware, and other groups known as the Purple party, the Pimple party, and the Outer party—each planning to enter the political framework of their respective communities. These seem to be new manifestations of movements like the Ranters, the Poor Conrads, and the Diggers that were mentioned earlier.

Those who demand the legalization of marijuana as well as those who speak of drug abuse step too easily into polar overgeneralizations. One cannot speak of the drug user without distinguishing the casual experimenter from the person who finds a new role in drug use, without recognizing the significant class difference between the speed freak (who is usually a lower-class slum adolescent) and a marijuana user (who is more likely to be college educated). Nor can we speak of response to drugs, in an effort to justify legalization, so long as evaluations of drug behavior are a consequence of the use of varying products with no standardization of control. Drug response will differ depending on whether one is using a homegrown weed in Nebraska or Missouri, in which the alleged effects are more likely to be simply euphoric, or whether one is using the concentrated products of Hawaii, India, or Vietnam. It makes a difference whether one takes a few drags off a roach passing around many hands at a party or whether one eats cookies spiked with high-grade Mexican marijuana that can toss one like a shuttlecock back and forth for hours.

Beside the standardization of dosage, personality factors, as well as the factors of psychological set and setting, all will determine the type of response an individual has. It is known, for example, that bad trips are more likely to result from a solitary user than from a group setting. To presume to make generalizations on the basis of contemporary experience seems to be unjustified. Many of the drugs on the street have been diverted from legitimate manufacturers but have been contaminated and changed. Still others have been produced by amateur do-it-yourself chemists in doses that vary and whose impurity can produce all kinds of side effects. Since no standardization of dose can be ascertained, we are still not in a position to say that the effects are generally benign.

In conclusion, what seems to be the major lesson to be learned about the drug culture is the need to realize its complexity and to avoid the implication of one polar position. In a generation that repudiated plastic culture, a new group of entrepeneurs has found status and upward mobility in the exploitation of the rags and patches of the new boutiques and in the flourishing music industry. If the culture has been used to improvise new forms of consumerism and to revitalize the consumer market, if it has served in its desublimation to support rather than to subvert the system, it has also served to reaffirm in some sections the need for community, the need for the resanctification of human relations and human experience.

The image of the "greening of America" seems to be too simple and too euphoric, but that view does at least emphasize some of the positive aspects that were a product of the new life-styles and the new culture. Yet the negative and destructive potentials still remain, and if we do not learn from history, we may again be destined to repeat it.

72 73 74 75 10 9 8 7 6 5 4 3 2 1